OPPOSING
VIEWPOINTS®
SERIES

# World Religion

# Other Books of Related Interest:

## Opposing Viewpoints Series
AIDS

The Catholic Church

Cloning

Culture Wars

Genetic Engineering

India and Pakistan

Iraq

Islam

Israel

The Middle East

Religion in America

## At Issue Series
AIDS in Developing Countries

Anti-Semitism

Creation versus Evolution

The Ethics of Genetic Engineering

The Ethics of Human Cloning

How Does Religion Influence Politics?

Is Islam a Religion of War or Peace?

Islam in America

Islamic Fundamentalism

The Israeli-Palestinian Conflict

Religion and Education

# "Congress shall make no law ... abridging the freedom of speech, or of the press."

*First Amendment to the U.S. Constitution*

The basic foundation of our democracy is the First Amendment guarantee of freedom of expression. The Opposing Viewpoints Series is dedicated to the concept of this basic freedom and the idea that it is more important to practice it than to enshrine it.

# OPPOSING VIEWPOINTS® SERIES

# World Religion

*Mike Wilson, Book Editor*

**GREENHAVEN PRESS**

*An imprint of Thomson Gale, a part of The Thomson Corporation*

Detroit • New York • San Francisco • New Haven, Conn. • Waterville, Maine • London • Munich

THOMSON
★
GALE
™

Bonnie Szumski, *Publisher*
Helen Cothran, *Managing Editor*

© 2006 Thomson Gale, a part of The Thomson Corporation.

Thomson and Star logo are trademarks and Gale and Greenhaven Press are registered trademarks used herein under license.

*For more information, contact:* Greenhaven Press
27500 Drake Rd.
Farmington Hills, MI 48331-3535
Or you can visit our Internet site at http://www.gale.com

LIBRARY OF CONGRESS CATALOGING-IN-PUBLICATION DATA

World religion / Mike Wilson, book editor.
     p. cm. -- (Opposing viewpoints)
     Includes bibliographical references and index.
     ISBN 0-7377-2969-4 (lib : alk. paper) -- ISBN 0-7377-2970-8 (pbk. : alk. paper)
     1. Religion. I. Wilson, Mike. II. Opposing viewpoints series (Unnumbered)
     BL25.W67 2007
     200--dc22
                                                                    2006041172

Printed in the United States of America
10 9 8 7 6 5 4 3 2 1

# Contents

Why Consider Opposing Viewpoints?                      11

Introduction                                           14

## Chapter 1: Can the World's Religions Solve Global Problems?

Chapter Preface                                        18

1. Religion Is Irrelevant in Most Modern Societies     20
   *Gregory S. Paul*

2. Religion Benefits Modern Societies                  28
   *The Dalai Lama*

3. The Catholic Church Helps Fight AIDS                33
   *H.E. Javier Cardinal Lozano Barragan*

4. The Catholic Church Undermines AIDS                 40
   Prevention Efforts
   *Charlotte Watts*

5. Faith-Based Initiatives Work Better than            47
   Secular Programs
   *George W. Bush*

6. Faith-Based Initiatives Do Not Work Better than     53
   Secular Programs
   *Amy Sullivan*

Periodical Bibliography                                59

## Chapter 2: Do the World's Religions Promote War?

Chapter Preface                                        61

1. Islam Encourages Wars of Aggression                63
   *Daniel Pipes*

2. Islam Does Not Encourage Wars of Aggression        69
   *John Esposito*

3. Christianity Forbids War                            78
   *John Dear*

4. Christianity Accepts Just Wars  84
  *James Turner Johnson*

5. Buddhism Forbids War  93
  *Mahinda Deegalle*

6. Buddhism Permits Defensive Wars  101
  *Tessa Bartholomeusz*

Periodical Bibliography  109

## Chapter 3: Are Religion and Science in Conflict?

Chapter Preface  111

1. Intelligent Design Is a Scientific Theory  114
  *Intelligent Design and Evolution Awareness Center*

2. Intelligent Design Is Unscientific  122
  *American Academy for the Advancement of Science*

3. Embryonic Stem Cell Research Fulfills Christians' Duty to Save Lives  129
  *Nancy Pelosi*

4. Embryonic Stem Cell Research Destroys Human Lives  134
  *William Saunders*

5. Spirituality Is Genetically Determined  139
  *Dean Hamer*

6. Evidence That Spirituality Is Genetically Determined Is Weak  148
  *Carl Zimmer*

Periodical Bibliography  154

## Chapter 4: Is Religious Fundamentalism a Serious Problem?

Chapter Preface  156

1. The Koran Permits Martyrdom Bombing  158
  *Yousef al-Qaradhawi*

2. The Koran Forbids Suicide Bombing     **164**
   *Bernard Lewis*

3. Christian Fundamentalism Threatens Democracy     **170**
   in the United States
   *Henry A. Giroux*

4. Christian Fundamentalism Promotes Moral     **177**
   Government in the United States
   *Shmuley Boteach*

5. Hindu Fundamentalism Threatens India     **185**
   *Amitabh Pal*

6. Hindu Fundamentalism Will Not Seriously     **195**
   Threaten India
   *Ashgar Ali Engineer*

7. Israeli Jewish Fundamentalists Promote Violence     **202**
   in the Middle East
   *David Hirst*

8. Israeli Jews Work for Peace in the Middle East     **211**
   *Liberal Judaism*

Periodical Bibliography     **216**

For Further Discussion     **217**

Organizations to Contact     **220**

Bibliography of Books     **224**

Index     **226**

# Why Consider Opposing Viewpoints?

> *"The only way in which a human being can make some approach to knowing the whole of a subject is by hearing what can be said about it by persons of every variety of opinion and studying all modes in which it can be looked at by every character of mind. No wise man ever acquired his wisdom in any mode but this."*
>
> *John Stuart Mill*

In our media-intensive culture it is not difficult to find differing opinions. Thousands of newspapers and magazines and dozens of radio and television talk shows resound with differing points of view. The difficulty lies in deciding which opinion to agree with and which "experts" seem the most credible. The more inundated we become with differing opinions and claims, the more essential it is to hone critical reading and thinking skills to evaluate these ideas. Opposing Viewpoints books address this problem directly by presenting stimulating debates that can be used to enhance and teach these skills. The varied opinions contained in each book examine many different aspects of a single issue. While examining these conveniently edited opposing views, readers can develop critical thinking skills such as the ability to compare and contrast authors' credibility, facts, argumentation styles, use of persuasive techniques, and other stylistic tools. In short, the Opposing Viewpoints Series is an ideal way to attain the higher-level thinking and reading skills so essential in a culture of diverse and contradictory opinions.

In addition to providing a tool for critical thinking, Opposing Viewpoints books challenge readers to question their own strongly held opinions and assumptions. Most people form their opinions on the basis of upbringing, peer pressure, and personal, cultural, or professional bias. By reading carefully balanced opposing views, readers must directly confront new ideas as well as the opinions of those with whom they disagree. This is not to simplistically argue that everyone who reads opposing views will—or should—change his or her opinion. Instead, the series enhances readers' understanding of their own views by encouraging confrontation with opposing ideas. Careful examination of others' views can lead to the readers' understanding of the logical inconsistencies in their own opinions, perspective on why they hold an opinion, and the consideration of the possibility that their opinion requires further evaluation.

## Evaluating Other Opinions

To ensure that this type of examination occurs, Opposing Viewpoints books present all types of opinions. Prominent spokespeople on different sides of each issue as well as well-known professionals from many disciplines challenge the reader. An additional goal of the series is to provide a forum for other, less known, or even unpopular viewpoints. The opinion of an ordinary person who has had to make the decision to cut off life support from a terminally ill relative, for example, may be just as valuable and provide just as much insight as a medical ethicist's professional opinion. The editors have two additional purposes in including these less-known views. One, the editors encourage readers to respect others' opinions—even when not enhanced by professional credibility. It is only by reading or listening to and objectively evaluating others' ideas that one can determine whether they are worthy of consideration. Two, the inclusion of such viewpoints encourages the important critical thinking skill of objectively evaluating an author's credentials and bias. This evaluation will illuminate an author's reasons for taking a particular stance on an issue and will aid in readers' evaluation of the author's ideas.

It is our hope that these books will give readers a deeper understanding of the issues debated and an appreciation of the complexity of even seemingly simple issues when good and honest people disagree. This awareness is particularly important in a democratic society such as ours in which people enter into public debate to determine the common good. Those with whom one disagrees should not be regarded as enemies but rather as people whose views deserve careful examination and may shed light on one's own.

Thomas Jefferson once said that "difference of opinion leads to inquiry, and inquiry to truth." Jefferson, a broadly educated man, argued that "if a nation expects to be ignorant and free . . . it expects what never was and never will be." As individuals and as a nation, it is imperative that we consider the opinions of others and examine them with skill and discernment. The Opposing Viewpoints Series is intended to help readers achieve this goal.

*David L. Bender and Bruno Leone,*
*Founders*

# Introduction

> *"All the great religions and traditions overlap when it comes to the fundamental principles of human conduct: charity, justice, compassion, mutual respect, [and] the equality of human beings in the sight of God."*
>
> —*Kofi Annan, United Nations Secretary-General*

The English word *religion* is derived from the Latin word *religio*, which refers to the awe or fear that is experienced in the presence of a god or spirit. Philosopher William James, in *The Varieties of Religious Experience*, says that religion "consists of the belief that there is an unseen order, and that our supreme good lies in harmoniously adjusting ourselves thereto." According to Adherents.com, there are more than forty-two hundred religions, both minor and major. Christianity is the largest religious group, with approximately 2.1 billion adherents, followed by Islam with 1.3 billion. Hinduism is third, with 900 million adherents; Chinese traditional religion is fourth, with 394 million; and Buddhism fifth, with 376 million. The sheer number of religions in the world begs the question: Why? Why are people so attracted to religious faith?

An obvious answer to this question is that people embrace religion because God exists and they need an avenue for understanding and worshipping him. Such a metaphysical assertion has been debated throughout the ages, with thinkers of all stripes weighing in without definitively settling the matter from a philosophical point of view. Perhaps an easier question to answer is how people benefit practically from religious belief. Many experts believe that faith provides numerous benefits, both physically and spiritually. As religious historian Jeffrey Webb notes, "Belief in miracles satisfies our inner sense of something larger than ourselves, some unfathomable power, that provides direction, purpose, and meaning to existence. In a chaotic world, we rely on God to help us make sense of tragedy, suffering, and despair." A study by Thomas Mulligan appearing in the *Southern Medical Journal* in 2002 found that

> Christian intercessory prayer appears to improve health outcomes in patients admitted to a [coronary care unit] and may improve survival in children with leukemia. Islamic-based psychotherapy appears to speed recovery from anxiety and depression in Muslims. Religion may also have a positive impact on immune function, blood pressure, depression, suicide rate, and mortality in older adults. . . .The preponderance of the evidence supports the beneficial effect of religion on health outcomes.

Although these benefits make it clearer why individuals are drawn to religion, many commentators note that religious faith has a dark side as well. ReligiousTolerance.org has identified wars and conflicts that have religious intolerance as an element in the following countries: Afghanistan, Ivory Coast, Cyprus, East Timor, India, Indonesia (two different provinces), Kashmir, Kosovo, Kurdistan, Macedonia, Middle East (Palestine and Israel), Nigeria, Northern Ireland, Pakistan, Philippines, Chechnya, South Africa, Sri Lanka, Sudan, Tibet, and Uganda. To that may be added Iraq, where Sunni and Shia sects of Islam are presently fighting each other in what threatens to become a civil war. Of the conflicts listed above, 87 percent involve Muslims, 61 percent involve Christians, and 57 percent involve conflicts between Christians and Muslims.

People of different religions, even when not at war, often show intense dislike, even hatred, toward each other. Indeed, adherents of one faith often disdain the religions of others. For example, the Reverend Franklin Graham has said that

Islam and Christianity do not worship the same God, that Islam has "a different God, and I believe [it is] a very evil and a very wicked religion." In 2002 the Reverend Jerry Falwell called the Islamic prophet Muhammad a terrorist, resulting in protests in India that caused eight deaths. In 2006, cartoons picturing Muhammad published in a Danish newspaper prompted riots in Europe and the Middle East. Muslims believe that no images of Muhammad must ever be shown and that the paper disrespected Islam by publishing the cartoons.

Many commentators believe that these kinds of conflicts are not actually religious in nature, however. As futurist Glen Hiemstra said in 2003, "The zealotry we see is mostly about money, power and land." People seeking personal wealth and power use religion to further their cause, these experts claim, giving religion a bad name. Moreover, many note, religion is often an agent of good. Indeed, churches often work to address poverty and disease around the world. Even considering the harms that religion can wreak, most people are drawn to religion anyway.

Debates over religion's role in world affairs and in people's personal lives will certainly continue. The authors in *Opposing Viewpoints: World Religion* contribute to the discussion in the following chapters: Can the World's Religions Help Solve Global Problems? Do the World's Religions Promote War? Are Religion and Science in Conflict? Is Religious Fundamentalism a Serious Problem? The viewpoints in this anthology provide the reader with an opportunity to form his or her own opinions about how religion affects the world today.

# CHAPTER 1

# Can the World's Religions Solve Global Problems?

# Chapter Preface

Global issues such as war, hunger, global warming, and terrorism are hard to address on a nation-by-nation basis. The problems are so complex, a united effort transcending national borders is often necessary if an effective solution is to be reached. Many commentators argue that the world's religions inspire people to work together to solve such problems. On the other hand, other analysts contend that religion works against solutions to global problems, and in some cases, helps create them.

Those who believe that religions unite people and inspire them to solve global problems assert that faith is a great motivator. Dirk Ficca, executive director of the Council for a Parliament of the World's Religions, notes, "When people of faith commit to address religious violence and other pressing issues facing the global community, they follow through. We make a commitment not only to the world, but out of a deeply rooted religious or spiritual conviction." Abdullah al-Truki, secretary-general of the Muslim World League, argues that Islam can solve problems such as drug abuse, poverty, insecurity, and moral degradation.

Indeed, history shows that religion can inspire followers to take action. Sulak Sivaraksa, a Buddhist social activist twice nominated for the Nobel Peace Prize, said he became an activist because of his desire "to truly follow the Buddha's teachings, and to make Buddhism relevant to modern society. It also had to do with a feeling of social responsibility. For instance, you don't steal. But if you let a few collect wealth at the expense of the poor, that is worse than stealing." Peace activist Father Roy Bourgeois, while in solitary confinement during his serving of a six-month sentence for participating in a political protest, wrote in 1997, "I have no regrets. More than ever, I feel that God calls each of us to be healers and peace makers. As the Apostle James said, we must integrate our faith with actions."

Even religious extremism has been seen as a positive force for social change. Civil rights activist Martin Luther King Jr., in his famous "Letter from Birmingham Jail," answered claims that he was a dangerous extremist thus: "We must never forget that all three [men crucified on Calvary] were crucified for the same crime—the crime of extremism. Two were extremists for immorality, and thus fell below their environment. The other, Jesus Christ, was an extremist for love, truth and goodness, and thereby rose above his environment." Many Americans see King as a hero who stood up for the rights of African Americans.

On the other hand, many analysts maintain that extreme religious beliefs often lead to disastrous results. Terrorists who attacked the United States on September 11, 2001, claimed to be engaged in a holy war and believed God would grant them paradise in the afterlife as a reward for killing nearly three thousand people. Adolph Hitler, the mastermind of the Nazi Holocaust, wrote in his autobiography, *Mein Kampf*, "I believe I am acting in accordance with the will of the Almighty Creator: by defending myself against the Jew, I am fighting for the work of the Lord."

Whether religion is a positive or negative force in the world continues to be debated vociferously. The authors in this chapter continue the discussion, focusing specifically on religion's role in solving global problems.

| "God may not be dead in the developed democracies, but in some of them he is on life support, and there is no sign of a revival."

# Religion Is Irrelevant in Most Modern Societies

*Gregory S. Paul*

*In this viewpoint Gregory S. Paul argues that, except in America, religious belief and practice has declined in all developed democracies, where ardent belief in God, he says, is viewed as peculiar. He claims that communism repressed religion in most nations where it gained power, further contributing to religion's decline. Affluence and education, he says, combine to make religion seem less relevant. Paul is an evolutionary scientist, paleontologist, and author of* Dinosaurs in the Air.

As you read, consider the following questions:

1. The work of what scientist, according to the author, has contributed greatly to the decline in religious belief?

2. According to the author, what country has the largest

percentage of agnostics and atheists?

3. Which country, according to the author, has the most nonbelievers in a higher power?

It is estimated that only a few million people were nonreligious in 1990. . . . Today the estimate is nearly one billion, a sixth of the world's population. This 250-fold expansion in absolute numbers and fifty-fold increase in percentage of population in just one long lifespan far outstrips the growth of any major faith in the twentieth century, and probably in history. According to the World Christian Encyclopedia, believers in the supernatural belong to 10,000 variations, most within ten major varieties of organized religion. Christianity's percentage of the population has remained remarkably stable, at about one in three, spread across some 34,000 denominations. If anything, the percentage of Christians has declined slightly during the past one hundred years. Among the major religions, only Islam has seen major growth: from about 12 percent of the global population in 1900 to nearly 20 percent today. In general, rising levels of education and income have corresponded to higher rates of religious skepticism in the modern world, in particular, most scientists are atheistic, and the degree of skepticism and/or secularism appears to have increased sharply among the most distinguished researchers.

One hundred years ago, nations varied little in their gross rate of religious belief; today a wide disparity exists. In countries other than developed democracies without a history of communist rule, rates of belief remain high and relatively little changed from the past. At least 80 percent of their populations remain absolute believers, with most of the rest being favorable to supernaturalism. This pattern verifies that low income and education levels are incompatible with high rates of rationalism, skepticism, and secularism. In many Islamic countries and in Hindu India, there has been a rise in fundamentalism, although this may be slacking off in countries such as Iran.

## Patterns in U.S.

The United States exhibits a broadly similar pattern, retaining high rates of basic supernatural belief. Nearly two-thirds of Americans profess an absolute belief in God, and more than nine out of ten are at least favorable to the existence of a higher power (a rate little changed in over fifty years). In many respects, Christian influence has grown during American history. Many early American leaders (Washington, Jefferson, Franklin, Allen, Paine, Lincoln) were non-Christian deists; it is doubtful whether such skeptics of the divinity of Christ could be elected in present-day America. Church membership has risen throughout our country's history from less than one in five in revolutionary times to greater than three in five today leading to quality-of-life protests over megachurch construction and expansion in many communities. In the later third of the 1900s, fundamentalism gained at the expense of less-conservative denominations. Today at least a third of Americans profess biblical-literalist Christian fundamentalism. A Gallup analysis of multiple indicators concludes that religious belief and practice rose in the 1990s after a long but modest decline that began in the 50s and 60s. Meanwhile, more than a third of Americans distrust nonbelievers; 70 percent consider them unsuitable mates.

However, the situation is not straightforward: for example, American tolerance for nonbelievers is growing, and absolute God-belief in the United States is already somewhat lower than in the Third World. Sundays have become homogenized with the rest of the week. Some surveys suggest that overall church affiliation and attendance has begun to decline. Strident religious conservatism may represent a desperate attempt to retain influence at a time when modern science and technology are undermining supernaturalism in fundamental ways.

## Agnostic/Atheist Percentages of Developed-World Populations

| | |
|---|---|
| France | 37% |
| Sweden | 35% |
| Japan | 31% |
| Denmark | 31% |
| Holland | 29% |
| England | 25% |
| Australia | 24% |
| Germany | 24% |
| Norway | 24% |
| New Zealand | 20% |
| Canada | 17% |
| Switzerland | 16% |
| Spain | 16% |
| Austria | 15% |
| Italy | 9% |
| United States | 8% |
| Ireland | 6% |
| Portugal | 5% |

*Gregory S. Paul,* Free Inquiry, *June 22, 2002.*

## Patterns in Other Developed Democracies

Communism successfully suppressed religious belief in most nations where it gained power. In once-czarist Russia, fewer than one in four are absolute believers in God, though this number may have doubled in the past decade. In eastern Germany since the fall of the Berlin Wall the percentage of absolute believers has held steady at about one in ten. It is the one (former) nation known to have a strong majority (two-thirds) of agnostics and other atheists who do not believe in a higher power. In contrast, Poland is unusual in remaining strongly Catholic.

The link between communism and atheism is well known. Yet neither has religion fared well in the West, aside from the United States. With the exception of America, all prosperous developed democracies have seen such dramatic declines in religious belief and practice that they can be labeled secular developed democracies. If we take these nations as a bloc, absolute believers in God and nonbelievers in a higher power each make up a quarter of the combined population. In none of the secular developed democracies does absolute belief in God exceed 50 percent. Historically Catholic Ireland, Italy and Spain are the least secular among these nations. At the other extreme are once-emperor-worshiping Japan, where a mere 4 percent (mostly Christians) now have an absolute belief in God; and the Scandinavian countries, where just 12 to 15 percent do. In absolute terms, Japan has the most nonbelievers in a higher power: about 40 million, outnumbering absolute believers in a creator 8 to 1. France has the largest percentage of agnostics and atheists, about two in five, outnumbering absolute believers 2 to 1, a ratio also seen in Sweden. Coverage of the 2000 Olympics revealed once-conservative Australia as a nation of hedonistic sport and beach worshipers. Even hyper-conservative Catholic Ireland (excluding the northern counties) saw a precipitous drop in religious belief and practice over the last decade, especially among the young.

None of the secular developed democracies is Christian in the sense that a majority of the population consists of devout believers in a divine Christ. Praying and other religious practices are correspondingly reduced. In these secular democracies ardent belief in God is widely considered peculiar, the fate of empty churches is a practical problem, and much of the clergy faces financial crisis. Few politicians fear to expose—or espouse—their lack of faith. . . .

Few in the secular developed democracies take the Bible literally; the great majority agree that humans descended from fossil apes. New Age beliefs have to some extent replaced

Christianity but even when this is taken into account, most secular developed democracies are strikingly naturalistic, rationalistic, and humanistic. God may not be dead in the developed democracies, but in some of them he is on life support, and there is no sign of a revival.

It is remarkable—and too little appreciated—that suddenly Europe is no longer a truly Christian continent. Instead, in conjunction with Canada, Japan, and Australia, it anchors history's greatest stronghold of humanistic secularism. In the land of its founding, the Middle East, Christianity abides only in fast-dwindling trace communities. As a dominant sociopolitical force, Christianity has undergone an epic movement from the Middle East to Europe, thence to the Americas south of the Canadian border, retaining only such modest Old World enclaves as Poland and assorted nondeveloped nations. American evangelicals are now trying to re-Christianize the Eastern hemisphere, but enjoying significant success only in sub-Saharan Africa. The high rates of religious belief and practice that Americans think normal are actually aberrant and primitive for a First World nation. . . .

## Reasons Religion Is Declining

It is clear that if not for the scientific and technological revolution of the last centuries, absolute belief in God would remain high. The impact of Charles Darwin's *On the Origin of Species by Natural Selection* (1859) cannot be overemphasized. Without Darwin's effective elimination of the need for a cognitive designer, there would be hundreds of millions fewer nonbeievers. Removal of the need for a creator inevitably promotes disbelief in an educated population, so it is not surprising that in the developed democracies we find a consistent negative correlation between increasing understanding of evolution on the one hand and religious belief and practice on the other. The most secular country sampled, Japan, exhibits the highest understanding of evolution while the uniquely theistic United

States ranks lowest on this variable. There is no documented case where a developed democracy's population is both well-versed in evolutionary science and high in theistic belief and practice, or vice versa—and it is unlikely that any exists. Numerous creationists and their organizations correctly recognize that to negate the societal power of noncreationism will require that they furnish scientific proof of the existence of a creator. Of course, this is not likely to occur.

Dramatic social changes of the last one hundred-odd years have driven secularization in the secular developed democracies. A century ago, most people lived lives not all that different from their ancestors. My one-hundred-year-old grandmother grew up in a central-Utah frontier town with no automobiles, radios, planes, or running water; phones and telegraphs were rare; her mother had lost nearly half of her children, a juvenile mortality rate typical of the time. Most urban dwellers lived in squalid tenement communities with few modern amenities. Few had ready access to sources of information that presented alternatives to the religious dogma predominant in their community.

Today in contrast, many inhabitants of developed democracies travel the world almost at will, returning to spacious homes filled with high-tech equipment that would dazzle Einstein. Access to abundant foods and advanced medical care means that they regularly live into their seventies and eighties. Perhaps most important, childhood death is extremely rare. Birth control and safe abortion allow sex to occur outside of sanctified marriage without the complication of pregnancy.

Living like pampered and protected demi-gods has undoubtedly allowed millions to discard belief in archaic myths. . . .

The common American view that religion is here to stay despite the advances of science and technology—promoted by many theists and often tacitly accepted even by skeptics—is an illusion fueled by most Americans' chronic provincialism. Few

Europeans and Japanese share this view. Instead, their clerics are beset by theistic panic. Obviously it is not only possible for advanced societies to achieve high rates of rationalism and secularism in a relatively short timeframe, it is normal for them to do so. Intensive propaganda campaigns are not required to achieve this effect. Although it may be true that humans are genetically programmed to engage in spiritual thought, the fact that large populations have so easily abandoned faith proves that cultural and intellectual influences are also vital, and can overcome such transcendental predispositions as exist.

> "Expanding [inner] peace . . . to the
> world will bring mutual trust, mutual
> respect, sincere communication, and
> finally successful joint efforts to solve
> the world's problems."

# Religion Benefits
# Modern Societies

### The Dalai Lama

*The Dalai Lama, winner of the 1989 Nobel Peace Prize and
spiritual leader of Tibetan Buddhism, argues in this viewpoint
that love, cultivated through religious practice, can benefit the
world. He argues that all religions teach love, and that cultivat-
ing love opens the heart to peace. Practicing love, he says, is the
real religion that leads people to serve, rather than dominate,
others.*

As you read, consider the following questions:

1. What are the real sources of happiness, in the author's
   view?

2. To what degree, says the author, can humans develop love?

3. Where is the "real" temple for religion, in the author's view?

When I speak about love and compassion, I do so not as a Buddhist, nor as a Tibetan, nor as the Dalai Lama. I do so as one human being speaking with another. I hope that you at this moment will think of yourself as a human being rather than as an American, Asian, European, African, or member of any particular country. These loyalties are secondary. If you and I find common ground as human beings, we will communicate on a basic level. If I say, "I am a monk," or "I am a Buddhist," these are, in comparison to my nature as a human being, temporary. To be human is basic, the foundation from which we all arise. You are born as a human being, and that cannot change until death. All else—whether you are educated or uneducated, young or old, rich or poor—is secondary.

## Love Overcomes Anger

In big cities, on farms, in remote places, throughout the countryside, people are moving busily. Why? We are all motivated by desire to make ourselves happy. To do so is right. However, we must keep in mind that too much involvement in the superficial aspects of life will not solve our larger problem of discontentment. Love, compassion, and concern for others are real sources of happiness. With these in abundance, you will not be disturbed by even the most uncomfortable circumstances. If you nurse hatred, however, you will not be happy even in the lap of luxury. Thus, if we really want happiness, we must widen the sphere of love. This is both religious thinking and basic common sense.

Anger cannot be overcome by anger. If a person shows anger to you, and you show anger in return, the result is a

## Religion as Peacemaker

While the religious causes of conflict receive plenty of public attention, the role of religious peacemakers tends to be neglected. Most faiths call on their members to be peacemakers, and increasing numbers of religious organizations are identifying opportunities to promote peace, even in situations where religion contributes to conflict.

*David Smock,* Harvard International Review, *January 1, 2004.*

disaster. In contrast, if you control your anger and show its opposite—love, compassion, tolerance, and patience—then not only will you remain in peace, but the anger of others also will gradually diminish. No one can argue with the fact that in the presence of anger, peace is impossible. Only through kindness and love can peace of mind be achieved.

Only human beings can judge and reason; we understand consequences and think in the long term. It is also true that human beings can develop infinite love, whereas to the best of our knowledge animals can have only limited forms of affection and love. However, when humans become angry, all of this potential is lost. No enemy armed with mere weapons can undo these qualities, but anger can. It is the destroyer.

If you look deeply into such things, the blueprint for our actions can be found within the mind. Self-defeating attitudes arise not of their own accord but out of ignorance. Success, too, is found within ourselves. Out of self-discipline, self-awareness, and clear realization of the defects of anger and the positive effects of kindness will come peace. For instance, at present you may be a person who gets easily irritated. However, with clear understanding and awareness, your irritability can first be undermined, and then replaced. . . .

## Religion Is Love

All religions teach a message of love, compassion, sincerity, and honesty. Each system seeks its own way to improve life for us all. Yet if we put too much emphasis on our own philosophy, religion, or theory, becoming too attached to it, and try to impose it on other people, the result will be trouble. Basically all the great teachers, including Gautama Buddha, Jesus Christ, Muhammad, and Moses, were motivated by a desire to help their fellow beings. They did not seek to gain anything for themselves, nor to create more trouble in the world.

Religion may have become synonymous with deep philosophical issues, but it is love and compassion that lie at the heart of religion. . . . Foolish selfish people are always thinking of themselves, and the result is always negative. Wise persons think of others, helping them as much as they can, and the result is happiness. Love and compassion are beneficial both for you and for others. Through your kindness toward others, your mind and heart will open to peace.

## Expanding Peace Worldwide

Expanding this inner environment to the larger community around you will bring unity, harmony, and cooperation; expanding peace further still to nations and then to the world will bring mutual trust, mutual respect, sincere communication, and finally successful joint efforts to solve the world's problems. All this is possible. But first we must change ourselves.

Each one of us is responsible for all of humankind. We need to think of each other as true brothers and sisters, and to be concerned with each other's welfare. We must seek to lessen the suffering of others. Rather than working solely to acquire wealth, we need to do something meaningful, something seriously directed toward the welfare of humanity as a whole.

## True Religion

Being motivated by compassion and love, respecting the rights of others—this is real religion. To wear robes and speak about God but think selfishly is not a religious act. On the other hand, a politician or a lawyer with real concern for humankind who takes actions that benefit others is truly practicing religion. The goal must be to serve others, not dominate them. Those who are wise practice love. As the Indian scholar and yogi Nagarjuna says in his *Precious Garland of Advice*:

> Having analyzed well All deeds of body, speech, and mind,
> Those who realize what benefits self and others And always
> do these are wise.

A religious act is performed out of good motivation with sincere thought for the benefit of others. Religion is here and now in our daily lives. If we lead that life for the benefit of the world, this is the hallmark of a religious life.

This is my simple religion. No need for temples. No need for complicated philosophy. Your own mind, your own heart, is the temple; your philosophy is simple kindness.

> "The Catholic Church continues to make her contribution both as regards prevention and in caring for people afflicted by HIV/AIDS."

# The Catholic Church Helps Fight AIDS

### H.E. Javier Cardinal Lozano Barragan

*H.E. Javier Cardinal Lozano Barragan is president of the Pontifical Council for Health Pastoral Care. In this viewpoint, which was taken from the Vatican's message for the December 1, 2005, World Day Against AIDS, he argues that the Catholic Church is actively involved in caring for people infected with HIV/AIDS. He also stresses the church's role in preventing AIDS. The best AIDS prevention, he argues, is confining sexual activity—which can transmit AIDS—to marriage in conformity with Catholic Church teachings.*

As you read, consider the following questions:

1. What percentage of centers for HIV/AIDS care worldwide are Catholic based?
2. Which of the Ten Commandments does the author say

*Vatican Message for the World Day Against AIDS*, 2005. Reproduced by permission of Libreria Editrice Vaticana.

is key to preventing AIDS?

3. How many people worldwide were living with AIDS in 2005, according to the author?

The World Day against AIDS of this year [2005], organized by UNAIDS, with the slogan "Stop AIDS. Keep the promise," seeks to call everyone, and in particular those who occupy positions of responsibility in the field of HIV/AIDS, to a renewed and conscious commitment to the lasting prevention of the spread of this pandemic and to care for those afflicted by it, especially in poor countries, in order to stem and invert the trend towards the growing spread of infection by HIV/AIDS.

The Pontifical Council for Health Pastoral Care joins with other national and international organizations, and in particular UNAIDS, which every year organizes a world campaign of combating AIDS, so that this planetary evil, which has brought about a global crisis, can be met with an action that is equally global and united. The adherence in 2001 of Heads of State and representatives of governments to the Declaration of commitment to the struggle against HIV/AIDS was an important moment of affirming awareness and political commitment at a world level in favour of a strong, global and decisive reaction and response by the international community.

The epidemiological situation of HIV/AIDS continues to rouse great concern. It is estimated that in 2005 the number of people living with AIDS was 40.3 million, of whom 2.3 million were minors under the age of fifteen. Year by year the number of people infected by this disease continues to grow. In 2005, 4.9 million people contracted the HIV virus, of whom 700,000 were minors under the age of fifteen, and in 2005, 3.1 million people died of AIDS, of whom 570,000 were young people under the age of fifteen. HIV/AIDS continues to sow death in all the countries of the world.

## Cure Through Prevention

The best cure is prevention to avoid infection by HIV/AIDS, which we should remember is transmitted through the triple route of blood, transmission from mother to child, and sexual contact. As regards transfusions and other forms of contact with the blood of an infected person, today such infection has been notably reduced. Despite this fact, the very greatest attention should be paid to avoid this pathway of infection, especially in centres that deal with transfusions and during surgical operations.

We may thank the Lord that contagion from mother to child is strongly controlled by suitable drugs. Prevention in this field must be intensified through the provision of suitable medication to seropositive mothers, especially by public bodies in the various countries of the world.

## Sexuality and AIDS

The third pathway of infection—sexual transmission—still remains the most important. This is greatly fostered by a kind of pansexual culture that devalues sexuality, reducing it to mere pleasure without any further meaning. Radical prevention in this field must come from a correct conception and practice of sexuality, where sexual activity is understood in its deep meaning as a total and absolute expression of the fecund giving of love. This totality leads us to the exclusiveness of its exercise in marriage, which is unique and indissoluble. Secure prevention in this field thus lies in the intensification of the solidity of the family.

This is the profound meaning of the Sixth Commandment[1], of the law of God, which constitutes the fulcrum of the authentic prevention of AIDS in the field of sexual activity.

1. The Sixth Commandment forbids adultery.

## Abstinence Works

[Uganda President Yoweri Museveni said:] "AIDS is mainly a moral, social, and economic problem" and that the best way to fight it is with "relationships based on love and trust, instead of institutionalized mistrust, which is what the condom is all about." The key to the drop in infections in Uganda was a delay in the average age of a woman's first sexual experience and a reduction in the number of her partners. Abstinence works.

*James K. Glassman, "Sex Religion, and AIDS"*
*American Enterprise Online. www.taemag.com.*

Faced with the difficult social, cultural and economic situation in which many countries find themselves, there can be no doubt that a defence and promotion of health is required that is a sign of the unconditional love of everyone, in particular for the poorest and the weakest, and which meets the human needs of every individual and the community. As a result those laws that do not take into sufficient consideration the equal distribution of conditions of health for everyone must be reformed. Health is a good in itself and we can say that "there weighs upon it a social mortgage."

Thus health must be assured to all the inhabitants of the earth and studies must be engaged in so that resources are used to achieve health for everyone by ensuring the basic care and treatment that are still denied to the majority of the population of the world. The right to the defence of health must, however, be matched by the duty to implement forms of behaviour and to follow lifestyles that are directed to defending health and to reject those that compromise health.

## The Church Cares for the Sick

The Catholic Church continues to make her contribution both as regards prevention and in caring for people afflicted by HIV/AIDS and their families at the level of medical care and assistance and at the social, spiritual and pastoral levels. 26.7% of centres for the provision of care in relation to HIV/AIDS in the world are Catholic based. Local Churches, religious institutions and lay associations have promoted very many projects and programs dealing with training and education, prevention and assistance, care and the pastoral accompanying of sick people, with love, a sense of responsibility, and a spirit of charity.

At a practical level, on the basis of the information that comes from the various local Churches and Catholic institutions in the world, the actions that are engaged in the field of AIDS may be categorized in the following way: the promotion of campaigns of sensitization, programs of prevention and health-care education, support for orphans, the distribution of medicaments and food, home care, the creation of hospitals, centres and therapeutic communities that concentrate their work around the provision of care and assistance for people afflicted by HIV/AIDS, working with governments, care in prisons, courses of catechesis, the creation of systems of help through Internet, and the establishment of support groups for sick people.

Flanking this inestimable and praiseworthy endeavour, on 12 September 2004 Pope John Paul II created the "Good Samaritan" Foundation, which was entrusted to the Pontifical Council for Health Pastoral Care and subsequently confirmed by Pope Benedict XVI, in order to bring economic help, thanks to the donations that are received, to the sick people who are most in need in the world, and in particular to the victims of HIV/AIDS. During this first year of activity of the Foundation significant financial help to purchase pharmaceuticals has been sent to the local Churches in America, Asia, Africa and Europe.

## Guidelines for Action

I would like to offer certain suggestions at the level of guidelines for action to those who are involved at various levels in the fight against HIV/AIDS:

- To Christian communities—that they may continue to promote the stability of the family and the education of children in a correct understanding of sexual activity as a gift of God for self-giving that is lovingly full and fertile.

- To governments—that they may promote the overall health of their populations and foster care for AIDS patients, basing themselves on the principles of responsibility, solidarity, justice and fairness.

- To the pharmaceutical industries—that they may facilitate economic access to anti-viral pharmaceuticals for the treatment of HIV/AIDS and those pharmaceuticals that are needed to treat opportunistic infections.

- To scientists and health-care workers—that they may renew their solidarity and do everything they can to advance biomedical research into HIV/AIDS in order to find new and effective pharmaceuticals that are able to stem the phenomenon.

- To the mass media—that they may provide transparent, correct and truthful information to populations on this phenomenon and on methods for its prevention, without forms of exploitation.

I would like to conclude with the words which Pope Benedict XVI addressed to the Bishops of South Africa during their "Ad Limina" visit on 10 June 2005: "Brother Bishops, I share your deep concern over the devastation caused by AIDS and related diseases. I especially pray for the widows, the orphans, the young mothers and those whose lives have been shattered by this cruel epidemic. I urge you to continue your efforts to fight this virus which not only kills but seriously threatens the economic and social stability of the Continent."

*"The Vatican undermines the vital work
of . . . many Catholics [fighting AIDS]
with its opposition to condom use."*

# The Catholic Church Undermines AIDS Prevention Efforts

## Charlotte Watts

*Charlotte Watts argues in this viewpoint that the Catholic Church disregards or distorts scientific information proving that condoms save lives by preventing HIV transmission. Moreover, she says, the Vatican uses its influence to encourage policy makers to discourage condom use. The church also discourages Catholics living in nations hit hard by AIDS from using condoms, thereby undermining the work of its own Catholic HIV/ AIDS care facilities. Watts is a member of the HIV Tools Research Group at the London School of Hygiene and Tropical Medicine.*

As you read, consider the following questions:

1. According to the author, what percentage of persons infected with HIV in sub-Saharan Africa is female?

Charlotte Watts, "The Ban that Kills: the Vatican's Allegations About Condoms Deny Scientific Facts and Costs Some People Their Lives," *Conscience*, March 22, 2005.

2. What is the annual failure rate for condom use, according to statistics cited by the author?

3. Why, according to Watts, does the Philippine Department of Health refuse to promote condom use?

When considering the Vatican's position on condoms, it is important to bear in mind the stark reality of the current AIDS epidemic. The Joint United Nations Programme on HIV/AIDS (UNAIDS) released figures on World AIDS Day estimating that there are between 36 and 44 million people infected with HIV/AIDS worldwide and about 14,000 new infections daily, mostly through heterosexual sex. Just under two-thirds of those living with HIV/AIDS are in Sub-Saharan Africa. Levels of HIV vary widely across the African subcontinent, with the prevalence of infection among adults aged 25–49 exceeding 35% in Swaziland and Botswana.

The high levels of HIV infection are driven by many factors including poverty, conflict, mobility and gender inequality. Women are now an increasing proportion of HIV infections. Societal, economic and biological gender inequalities— such as men choosing younger sexual partners and women often facing sexual violence and coercion—result in women being at increased risk of HIV infection compared to men. This is particularly apparent among young women in Sub-Saharan Africa where 57% of all people infected are women and girls, and more than three-quarters of young people infected are female.

There are also rapidly growing epidemics in parts of Asia and Eastern Europe. India is second only to South Africa in having the highest number of people living with HIV/AIDS. In many countries where HIV prevalence is fairly low, HIV infection is primarily concentrated in the groups most vulnerable to infection such as sex workers and injecting drug users. For example, data from sites in Vietnam, Indonesia and China indicate that 31–64% of injecting drug users and 7–16% of sex workers are HIV-infected. As the epidemic progresses, the sexual networks beyond these encounters also put regular partners at risk. Indeed, in some settings a large proportion of HIV infections now occur in regular partnerships. For example, in Cambodia in 2002, 60% of infections were between spouses where one was previously at risk through buying or selling sex. Likewise, more than 20% of infections in Honduras (2002), Kenya (1998) and Russia (2002) are from non-casual sex with a partner at risk. Several epidemiological studies find marriage to be the main risk factor of infection for women. For example, a study of married monogamous women in India concluded that it is likely that these women were being infected by their spouses. Despite this widespread and growing risk, few people around the globe know their HIV status, and many are not even aware that they are at risk, or lack knowledge of how to protect themselves from HIV. . . .

## Condoms Save Lives

The condom is a life-saving device: it is highly effective in preventing HIV transmission if used correctly and consistently, and is the best current method of HIV prevention for those who are sexually active and at risk. A review from the US National Institutes for Health concluded that condoms are protective against HIV infection, reducing the annual rate of HIV infection in sero-discordant couples (where only one partner is infected and risk of infection to the other is high) by 85% when used consistently. The efficacy of the condom per sex act will be even higher than this annual rate.

There is growing evidence that HIV prevention interventions can achieve substantial increases in levels of condom use in commercial and casual sex partnerships. Surveys of sex workers in Asia generally find that many—often over 70%—used condoms when they last had sex with a client. Sex workers in Sub-Saharan Africa can also attain high levels of consistent condom use with their clients. In some cases this rise in condom use clearly mirrors the declining levels of HIV infection. . . . HIV prevalence among sex workers who were first time attendees at a STI/AIDS testing clinic decreased as the consistency of condom use increased.

## Selective Interpretation of Data

The evidence on the condom's effectiveness is turned the other way round by Cardinal [Alphonso Lopez] Trujillo[1] who, instead of highlighting the protection provided, focuses on condoms' (annual) 15% failure rate in order to dissuade people from using them. Yet, perfection is not needed for a method to be immensely effective. Much in real life is not perfect—but the condom has a high effectiveness rate and the blunt fact is that, whether you see the glass as 85% full or 15% empty, if a person is going to have sex it is much better to use a condom than not to use one. Of course, some people may be in a position to choose and be able to remain abstinent until finding a lifetime partner who has also remained abstinent (and both have avoided HIV infection). However, banning condoms outright offers no possibility of protection for those who cannot or do not choose this lifestyle.

Cardinal Trujillo supports his argument that condoms do not protect against HIV by citing examples where HIV/AIDS cases increased as the number of condoms distributed also increased, and argues that as there is a much lower HIV prevalence in the Philippines (where there is strong opposition to the condom program by the church and a number of government leaders) than in Thailand (where a 100% condom use program was implemented for commercial sex), then condoms must not be effective. This is a selective interpretation of the data. We would hope that as HIV prevalence and general awareness of HIV/AIDS increase, condom demand, distribution and use would also increase. The HIV prevalence in a

1. Trujillo is president of the Vatican's Pontifical Council for the Family.

population can only decrease as people die or as new unin-fected people move into or are born into that population. This means that there may be a time-delay between condom use increasing and the effects of this on HIV prevalence being observed. Broad-brush comparisons between countries, such as Cardinal Trujillo made, are misleading. HIV epidemics are at different stages and of different types in different countries, and we should not draw over-simplistic conclusions about the reasons for this. Some suggest that the Philippines is on the verge of an HIV epidemic, while Thailand had to tackle its HIV epidemic much earlier. In fact, a major epidemic was probably averted through Thailand's strong provision of con-doms for commercial sex (starting in 1990).

Levels of awareness and correct knowledge of condoms, and their use, are also likely impeded by the Vatican perpetuat-ing untruthful anti-condom myths. As Cardinal Godfried Danneels said, when rebuking Cardinal Lopez Trujillo for his statements about condoms failing to protect against HIV, "it does not benefit a cardinal to deal with the virtue [scientific integrity] of a product." It is irresponsible of the Vatican to dismiss or misrepresent this scientific evidence that has been produced by leading international and scientific agencies, which clearly demonstrates that condoms, when used correctly and consistently, are highly effective at preventing HIV transmission.

## The Church Impedes Access to Condoms

There has been criticism that HIV prevention has traditionally focused extensively on condoms. Cardinal Trujillo seems to hold the view that many who promote condoms do so in a vacuum—devoid of all other options. Yet the popular AIDS education messages of recent times promote first abstinence then faithfulness or partner reduction, and then condoms. The enormity and complexity of the HIV epidemic means there are no easy solutions. The general consensus is, however,

## The Church's Stance

"The church says one must be faithful in marriage and save oneself for marriage," [said] the bishop of Thies in Senegal, Alexandre Mbengue. . . .

"We cannot say to people, to our youth, to all those who want to use condoms: 'Go ahead, use them' and thus cave in to the current trend," he said.

According to the [United Nations] agency UNAIDS, sub-Saharan Africa is hardest hit by AIDS, being home to more than two-thirds of those infected with HIV or full-blown AIDS worldwide—29.4 million out of 42 million.

Nevertheless, the church "cannot condone the use of condoms—indeed, we are campaigning against just that," said the archbishop of Lagos, Anthony Okogie, recently named a cardinal by [the late] Pope John Paul II.

*Coumba Sylla*, Agence France-Presse, *October 9, 2003.*
*www.aegis.com.*

that condoms do have an important part to play in a comprehensive response to the HIV epidemic.

When somebody holding strong socially or religiously conservative views also wields influence over national legislation, they can control the channeling of funds away from certain HIV/AIDS prevention programs, for example those that promote and distribute condoms. In addition, if some people's lifestyles, such as sex workers and homosexuals, are deemed to be illegal, it not only increases the stigma and discrimination these groups face but may also drive them away from accessible AIDS education and prevention services.

Particularly in settings where Catholicism is the predominant religion, the institutional church may limit the extent to which people are able to access condoms and also influence whether or not they are used. . . .

The prominent concerns in the AIDS prevention arena are the Vatican's opposition to condoms and its ability to sway national and international policies that subsequently impact on HIV/AIDS prevention strategies and services. Examples range from Brazil in the late 1980s when any AIDS prevention material mentioning condoms was vetoed and more recently with the banning of artificial contraception in Manila. In May 2004, Human Rights Watch published a report stating that the government of the Philippines "impedes access to condoms," crippling the work of HIV/AIDS service providers. The reason given by the Philippine Department of Health for refusing to promote condoms was "fear of offending conservative Catholics."

Polls consistently show that most Catholics disagree with the hierarchy's ban on condoms. Yet the same hierarchy that controls 100,000 hospitals and 200,000 other social service agencies worldwide ban both education about and the provision of condoms in their institutions. This attitude towards condoms is in sad contrast to the important contribution the church makes to the provision of AIDS care. Catholic organizations provide some 25% of AIDS care worldwide, making the Catholic church the largest institution in the world providing direct AIDS care. Ironically, the Vatican undermines the vital work of these many Catholics with its opposition to condom use.

> *"Rather than fear faith-based programs, welcome them. They're changing America. They do a better job than government can do."*

# Faith-Based Initiatives Work Better than Secular Programs

*George W. Bush*

*The following viewpoint was taken from remarks given by President George W. Bush on June 1, 2004, at the first White House National Conference on Faith-Based Community Initiatives. In it Bush argues that religion helps those in need more than government can. Faith-based groups should be given federal funds, he says, because such programs get results. He adds that federal funding of faith-based groups does not violate the constitutional mandate to separate church and state so long as the groups do not discriminate or proselytize.*

As you read, consider the following questions:

1. How many faith-based and community groups have been made aware that the federal government wants their help, according to the author?

George W. Bush, "Remarks to the White House National Conference On Faith-Based and Community Initiatives," June 1, 2004.

2. How frequently do miracles take place in America, in the author's view?

3. How many inmates did the author say would be released back into society in 2004?

I believe it is in the national interest that government stand side by side with people of faith who work to change lives for the better. I understand in the past some in government have said government cannot stand side by side with people of faith. Let me put it more bluntly, government can't spend money on religious programs simply because there's a rabbi on the board, cross on the wall or a crescent on the door. I view this as not only bad social policy—because policy bypassed the great works of compassion and healing that take place—I viewed it as discrimination. And we need to change it. . . .

I'm proud to report that we've reached more than 10,000 faith-based and community groups with the message that, "We want your help, that the federal government now welcomes your work, and do not fear being discriminated against by the government." . . .

Listen, what I'm telling you is that I've told our government—the people in my government, "Rather than fear faith-based programs, welcome them. They're changing America. They do a better job than government can do." . . .

## The Limits of Government

See, I understand the limitations of government. Governments can hand out money, but governments cannot put love in a person's heart or a sense of purpose in a person's life. The truth of the matter is that comes when a loving citizen puts their arm around a brother and sister in need and says, "I love you and God loves you, and together we can perform miracles." And miracles happen all the time in America. They happen because loving souls take time out of their lives to spread compassion and love.

And lives are changing. Listen, our society is going to change one heart and one soul at a time. It changes from the bottom up, not the top down. It changes when the soldiers in the armies of compassion feel wanted, encouraged and empowered. And that's what the faith-based and community initiative is all about.

How do we gather up the strength of the country, the vibrancy of faith-based programs, the social entrepreneurs? How do we encourage them? . . .

## Getting Results

America changes one heart at a time, one soul at a time. And while our fellow citizens can't do everything, they can do something to help change America one soul at a time. That's the philosophy behind the faith-based group. It is the government's strong desire to empower this fabric, this social fabric of our society, where faith-based programs large and small feel empowered, encouraged, and welcomed into changing lives.

Look, I fully understand it's important to maintain the separation of church and state. We don't want the state to become the church, nor do we want the church to become the state. We're on common agreement there. But I do believe that groups should be allowed to access social service grants so long as they don't proselytize or exclude somebody simply because they don't share a certain faith. In other words, there are ways to accomplish the separation of church and state and at the same time accomplish the social objective of having America become a hopeful place and a loving place.

So the question this administration is starting to ask, or is asking, is "Are you getting the results?" That's all we care about. Are you meeting the standards of church and state, and are you getting results? And if so, if you say, yes, the federal government, rather than being fearful of you, ought to say thank you; thank you for doing your mission to change the United States of America.

## Living Faith in the Public Square

"There is no contradiction between support for faith-based initiatives and upholding our constitutional principles," said [Senator Hillary] Clinton, a New York Democrat who often is mentioned as a possible presidential candidate in 2008. . . . She said there must be room for religious people to "live out their faith in the public square."

*Michael Jonas*, Boston Globe, *January 20, 2005.*

So I want to make sure that the faith-based groups simply got equal access and equal treatment when it came to the billions of dollars we spend at the federal level. That was the first step toward making sure the faith-based initiative was strong and vibrant. . . .

So we're making progress. I'm here to give you a progress report. They spent $1.1 billion on grants to faith-based groups. It's kind of hard to fully account for it. I would call that an estimate. $1.1 billion; it's an increase of 15 percent over 2002. That's good progress. However, there's a lot more money available. . . .

## Addiction and Mentoring

I have called upon—not only do we want to make sure that the monies being spent now are accessible to the faith community, but we want to make sure that—I've called for some specific programs to help the faith community.

One is called Access To Recovery. It is a $100 million initiative to help the addict is what it is. It's an interesting approach to funding social programs. In this case, we actually fund the addict. In other words, the money goes to the addict and the addict gets to choose the program that is best for her or him.

It's a change in attitude. Generally, we tend to fund the program, oftentimes not asking whether it's effective or not. This time we're sending the money to the addict so that the addict can make the decision that meets his or her needs. I will tell you, I will tell you: the cornerstone of any good recovery program is the understanding there is a higher being to whom you can turn your life, and therefore save your life. It is the crux of many, many a successful addiction program. And our government ought to understand that. Congress needs to provide ample money to the Access to Recovery Initiative to help addicts change their lives, by saving their lives.

I am deeply concerned about a society in which many boys and girls need love. They need—and I mentioned to you my concern about a child whose mom or dad is in prison. Got to be incredibly lonely to have your mom or dad in prison, wondering whether or not—you know, just wonder whether there's any hope, you know. And there is hope, particularly when that child feels love.

And so I've asked Congress to provide money for mentoring programs, particularly for a child whose mom or dad is in prison. And many of those mentoring programs come right out of inner-city churches and suburban churches. Listen, some of the best mentoring programs in America happen out of our churches and synagogues and mosques. And we ought not to be afraid of funding those programs. I mean, after all, if you exist because you've heard the universal call to love a neighbor like you'd like to be loved yourself, if that is the creed, the cornerstone, then surely out of that organization will come people who are willing to do so.

And part of loving your neighbor like you'd like to be loved yourself is mentoring a child, and saying, "You may be lonely, but I love you. And what can I do to help lift your spirit?" So I put in funding requests for programs such as this. More than 600,000 inmates will be released from prison this year. Those are a lot of souls that need help coming into our society. I can't think of a better place for a prisoner to go is to a church or synagogue or mosque and say, "I need help. I have just come out of incarceration, and can you help me with my life and the future? Can you provide guidance for me?"

And so we've got a $300 million initiative[1] I put before Congress to help with these prisoner reentry programs, all of which will give our faith community a chance to heal the broken heart. . . .

I'm telling America we need to not discriminate against faith-based programs. We need to welcome them so our society is more wholesome, more welcoming and more hopeful for every single citizen.

1. The Dept. of Labor announced on April 20, 2005, that $19.8 million in grants would be awarded to faith-based and community organizations under the President's Prisoner Reentry Program.

> *"There is no evidence that faith-based organizations work better than their secular counterparts; and, in some cases, they are actually less effective."*

# Faith-Based Initiatives Do Not Work Better than Secular Programs

*Amy Sullivan*

*Amy Sullivan argues in the following viewpoint that there is no evidence to support the claim that faith-based social programs work better than do secular programs. She contends that the federal government does not require evaluation of faith-based organizations receiving federal grants. According to Sullivan, the Bush administration is more concerned with funneling tax dollars to churches than determining such programs' effectiveness. Private studies, she argues, conclude that faith-based organizations are either equally or less effective at delivering social services than are secular programs. Amy Sullivan is an editor for Wash-ington Monthly.*

Amy Sullivan, "Faith Without Works: After Four Years, The President's Faith-Based Policies Have Proven to Be Neither Compassionate Nor Conservative," *Washington Monthly*, October 1, 2004, Copyright 2004 by Washington Monthly Publishing, LLC. Reproduced by permission.

As you read, consider the following questions:

1. Faith-based initiative successes in what state, says the author, were cited by the president in support of faith-based initiatives on the federal level?

2. According to sources cited by the author, what sort of evidence did the White House rely upon to support faith-based initiatives?

3. According to the Ford Foundation study cited by the author, which was better, faith-based job training programs or secular programs, at placing people in jobs?

When George W. Bush first hit the national political scene in the crowded field for the 2000 Republican nomination, what made him different, what made even liberal Americans take a second look, was his declaration that he was a "compassionate conservative." Unlike the flinty old conservatives of the past, Bush explained, a compassionate conservative would not be afraid to harness the power of government to minister to the unfortunate. But unlike traditional liberal Democrats, who relied on fumbling government bureaucracies, a compassionate conservative would empower and fund the charitable sector, particularly religious groups, to help those in need.

This breakthrough political slogan was embodied by a "faith-based initiative" that Bush talked about incessantly on the campaign trail and rolled out within the first month of taking over the White House. And Bush's image as a different kind of Republican was only reinforced by the tableau of black pastors, conservative evangelical leaders, and liberal crusaders for social justice who gathered around him as he introduced his faith-based domestic policy. The first part of the initiative sought to make it easier for religious organizations to get government grants to provide social services. Trumpeting the success of faith-based groups in Texas that ran drug rehabilitation and prison counseling programs, Bush argued that religious organizations could outperform their secular equivalents and so should be allowed to compete for the same government funds. . . .

Four years later, Bush's compassionate conservatism has turned out to be neither compassionate nor conservative. The policy of funding the work of faith-based organizations has, in the legacy of slashed social service budgets, devolved into a small pork-barrel program that offers token grants to the religious constituencies in [presidential political advisor] Karl Rove's electoral plan for 2004 while making almost no effort to monitor their effectiveness. . . .

## No Evaluation

From the very beginning, Bush has argued that faith-based groups should be judged on their results, and he insists that they do work better. The difference, he contends, is that they do more than simply minister to physical needs. On the campaign trail in the summer of 2000, Bush told audiences that religious organizations succeed where others fail "because they change hearts, they convince a person to turn their life over to Christ. Whenever my administration sees a responsibility to help people," he promised, "we will look first to faith-based organizations that have shown their ability to save and change lives." Bush had little empirical evidence to back up the claim that religious organizations were more effective. But he relentlessly talked of two seemingly-promising programs that the Texas state government had supported while he was governor. One was Teen Challenge, a drug rehabilitation program that claimed an astonishing 86 percent success rate. The other was InnerChange, a counseling program for prisoners that boasted impressively low levels of recidivism among its graduates. Certain critics raised questions about the reliability of the studies that produced these figures. But Bush kept repeating the claims, and most of the press corps passed them along uncritically. . . .

Critics worried that faith-based groups would be unduly privileged in the newly expanded grant-making world. For them, Bush had one word: results, results, results. In an interview with the religious Web site Beliefnet, he was asked whether he would support government money going to a Muslim group that taught prisoners the Koran. "The question I'd be asking," Bush replied, "is what are the recidivism rates? Is it working? I wouldn't object at all if the program worked." Four more times in the interview, Bush mentioned "results," noting that instead of promoting religion, "I'm promoting lower recidivism rates, and we will measure to make sure that's the case."

This rhetoric matched the administration's focus in other policy areas—like education—on accountability. Conservatives traditionally criticize government programs for throwing good money after bad, rewarding those who have not proven themselves effective with hard numbers like higher test scores, lower poverty rates, or reduced recidivism. Mel Martinez, Secretary of Housing and Urban Development, echoed the results-oriented sentiment in December 2002, telling an audience that "faith-based organizations should be judged on one central question: Do they work?" Conservatives thought they already knew the answer. "The fact is, we don't just suspect that faith-based programs work best," said [political commentator] Tucker Carlson on "Crossfire," "we know it."

Actually, we knew no such thing. But now we've had four years to measure results and reach a conclusion. Unfortunately, in the midst of all of the instructions included in the various executive orders, it turns out that the Bush administration forgot to require evaluation of organizations that receive government grants. According to a study released by the Pew-funded Roundtable on Religion and Social Welfare Policy in August 2004, "while more elaborate scientific studies are underway, the White House has relied on largely anecdotal evidence to support the view that faith-based approaches produce better long-term results." The accountability president has chosen not to direct any money toward figuring out whether faith-based approaches really work.

## The Evidence Is Negative

So it's a good thing that some academics and private organizations have picked up the slack. In the last few years, a few studies have looked at both faith-based and secular social service providers, and they have particularly tried to replicate the incredible results boasted by the model Texas programs. The verdict? There is no evidence that faith-based organizations work better than their secular counterparts; and, in some cases, they are actually less effective. In one study funded by the Ford Foundation, investigators found that faith-based job training programs placed only 31 percent of their clients in full-time employment while the number for secular organizations was 53 percent. And Teen Challenge's much ballyhooed 86 percent rehabilitation rate falls apart under examination—the number doesn't include those who dropped out of Teen Challenge and relies on a disturbingly small sample of those graduates who self-reported whether they had remained sober, significantly tilting the results.

It will take several more years to rigorously scrutinize the relative abilities of faith-based and secular organizations to provide effective social services, so it is impossible to know whether these initial findings are true across the board. And maybe in a perfect world it would be worth testing Bush's hunch and giving faith-based groups access to funds in the effort to alleviate poverty and other social problems. The problem is that, under the Bush administration, the overall pot of money for social services has shrunk considerably. This means that well-established organizations that have provided services for decades are now competing with—and, in some cases, being displaced by—unproven, often less-successful groups, inflicting a double whammy upon the people who really need the help. . . .

## The Real Goal

[T]he new faith-based grant program seems to have devolved into a religious version of race-based set-aside programs. As *The American Prospect* first reported last spring [2003], some states that are responsible for dispersing federal social service grants have altered their grant applications to include a box that potential grantees should check to indicate whether they are faith-based. In Massachusetts, several long-time recipients of funds for programs to help veterans learned the hard way that failure to check that box leads to the sudden denial of cash. When they identified themselves as "faith-based" the next time around, their applications were, not surprisingly, approved.

Some Bush officials are alarmingly honest about this quota-like system. When I asked Courtney McCormick, deputy director of the Department of Agriculture's faith-based office, what steps the administration is taking to track the effectiveness of faith-based grantees, she candidly replied, "That's not our concern." What they do care about, she said, is "getting more churches and community groups through the door to get access to funding."

# Periodical Bibliography

The following articles have been selected to supplement the diverse views in this chapter:

Stanley W.
Carlson-Thies

"Implementing the Faith-Based Initiatives,"
*Public Interest*, March 22, 2004.

Bruce Flamm

"The Columbia University 'Miracle' Study:
Flawed and Fraud," *Skeptical Inquirer*,
September 1, 2004.

Tom Frame

"God's Premature Obituaries," *Quadrant*, 2005.

Lee Hong Jung

"Healing and Reconciliation as the Basis for
the Sustainability of Life: An Ecological Plea
for a 'Deep' Healing and Reconciliation,"
*International Review of Mission*, January 1,
2005.

Diane E. Lewis

"Religion Finding Place on the Job," *Boston
Globe*, February 1, 2005.

Pamela Paul

"The Power to Uplift: Religious People Are
Less Stressed and Happier than Nonbelievers.
Research Is Beginning to Explain Why," *Time*,
January 17, 2005.

Tim Radford

"Study Refutes Faith in Silent Majority," *Guardian* (Manchester, UK), August 16, 2005.

Mary Ellen
Schoonmaker

"No Religion Has a Monopoly on Violence,"
*Hackensack (NJ) Record*, March 16, 2006.

# CHAPTER 2

# Do the World's Religions Promote War?

# Chapter Preface

The language of peace can be found in the scriptures and practices of most religions. For example, Muslims are taught to greet each other by saying *as-salaam alaykum* —"peace be upon you." Their daily prayers also end with the same phrase. Buddhism teaches that no sentient creature should be injured. Jesus instructed his followers to love their neighbors and to love not only friends but also persecutors.

Despite religious talk of peace, the language of war also appears in religious teachings. The Old Testament is filled with wars that the Hebrew God Yahweh commanded, and the New Testament Book of Revelation predicts a terrible war before the return of Christ. The Koran says that Allah helped Muslims, though outnumbered, to defeat their enemies. The Bhagavad Gita, a Hindu holy book that instructs one to live to achieve the highest spiritual realization, begins as Arjuna the warrior is about to engage in battle.

Not only is war referred to in holy writings, but many actual wars and conflicts have been fought in the name of religion. A prominent example of such a conflict is the Israeli-Palestinian struggle over Palestine. While obviously a conflict over land, the struggle is often seen in religious terms, as Muslims against Jews. Another example is terrorist Osama bin Laden and other militant Muslims, who have declared a jihad or "holy war" against the infidels (non-Muslims). Many experts warn that wars involving religion are especially difficult to resolve. In the words of Datuk Seri Dr. Mahathir bin Mohamad, then prime minister of Malaysia, addressing the World Evangelical Fellowship on May 4, 2001,

> Once started, religious strife has a tendency to go on and on, to become permanent feuds. Today we see such intractable inter-religious wars in Northern Ireland, between Jews and Muslims and Christians in Palestine, Hindus and

Muslims in South Asia and in many other places. Attempts to bring about peace have failed again and again. Always the extremist elements, invoking past injustices, imagined or real, will succeed in torpedoing the peace efforts and bringing about another [war] born of hostility.

Some analysts contend that religion itself is the cause of war. Sam Harris, author of *The End of Faith: Religion, Terror and the Future of Reason*, observes that "the central tenet of every religious tradition is that all others are mere repositories of error or, at best, dangerously incomplete. Intolerance is thus intrinsic to every creed." Professor Richard Dawkins of Oxford University has said that "religion is today's most divisive label of group identity and hostility. If a social engineer set out to devise a system for perpetuating our most vicious enmities, he could find no better formula than sectarian education."

Despite harsh criticism of religion, however, most people in the world are religious and say that religious teachings are deeply important to them. Holy writings inform their behavior, they assert, and their faith guides them in living a good life. Many commentators say that religion is indeed a positive force in the world and that corrupt leaders merely use it to divide people and win support for conflicts that are really about worldly gains such as land, money, and power. The authors in this chapter continue the debate over whether religion promotes war.

"*The purpose of jihad [holy war] is political, not religious. It aims not so much to spread the Islamic faith as to extend sovereign Muslim power.*"

# Islam Encourages Wars of Aggression

*Daniel Pipes*

*In this viewpoint Daniel Pipes contends that those claiming that jihad, or holy war, is a personal struggle against evil or a conflict waged in self-defense are being disingenuous. Muslims have promoted jihad for centuries to justify aggressive wars against non-Muslims and Muslims considered impious. The goal of jihad, he argues, is to replace all other faiths with Islam and establish an Islamic imperial world state. Pipes is the director of the Middle East Forum and author of* Militant Islam Reaches America.

As you read, consider the following questions:

1. How many of the seventy-eight battles fought by Muhammad were, according to the author, defensive?

2. According to Pipes, which variant of jihad was rarely mentioned in writings prior to the modern age?

3. How many of the 199 references to jihad in the most important collection of hadith called Sahib al-Bukhari refer to armed warfare against non-Muslims, according to the author?

Last spring [2002], the faculty of Harvard College selected a graduating senior named Zayed Yasin to deliver a speech at the university's commencement exercises in June. When the title of the speech "My American Jihad" —was announced, it quite naturally aroused questions. Why, it was asked, should Harvard wish to promote the concept of jihad—or "holy war" —just months after thousands of Americans had lost their lives to a jihad carried out by nineteen suicide hijackers acting in the name of Islam? Yasin, a past president of the Harvard Islamic Society, had a ready answer. To connect jihad to warfare, he said, was to misunderstand it. Rather, "in the Muslim tradition, jihad represents a struggle to do the right thing." [His] own purpose, Yasin added, was to "reclaim the word for its true meaning, which is inner struggle." . . .

The truth is that anyone seeking guidance on the all-important Islamic concept of jihad would get almost identical instruction from members of the professoriate across the United States. As I discovered through an examination of media statements by such university-based specialists, they tend to portray the phenomenon of jihad in a remarkably similar fashion—only, the portrait happens to be false.

## Jihadists Know Islam's History

The trouble with this accumulated wisdom of the scholars is simple to state. It suggests that [terrorist] Osama bin Laden had no idea what he was saying when he declared jihad on the United States several years ago and then repeatedly murdered Americans in Somalia, at the U.S. embassies in East

Africa, in the port of Aden, and then on September 11, 2001. It implies that organizations with the word "jihad" in their titles, including Palestinian Islamic Jihad and bin Laden's own "International Islamic Front for the Jihad Against Jews and Crusade[rs]," are grossly misnamed. And what about all the Muslims waging violent and aggressive jihads, under that very name and at this very moment, in Algeria, Egypt, Sudan, Chechnya, Kashmir, Mindanao, Ambon, and other places around the world? Have they not heard that jihad is a matter of controlling one's anger?

But of course it is bin Laden, Islamic Jihad, and the jihadists worldwide who define the term, not a covey of academic apologists. More importantly, the way the jihadists understand the term is in keeping with its usage through fourteen centuries of Islamic history.

## Jihad Is Islamic Domination

In premodern times, jihad meant mainly one thing among Sunni Muslims, then as now the Islamic majority. It meant the legal, compulsory, communal effort to expand the territories ruled by Muslims (known in Arabic as dar al-Islam) at the expense of territories ruled by non-Muslims (dar al-harb). In this prevailing conception, the purpose of jihad is political, not religious. It aims not so much to spread the Islamic faith as to extend sovereign Muslim power (though the former has often followed the latter). The goal is boldly offensive, and its ultimate intent is nothing less than to achieve Muslim dominion over the entire world.

By winning territory and diminishing the size of areas ruled by non-Muslims, jihad accomplishes two goals: it manifests Islam's claim to replace other faiths, and it brings about the benefit of a just world order. In the words of Majid Khadduri of Johns Hopkins University, writing in 1955 (before political correctness conquered the universities), jihad is "an instrument for both the universalization of [Islamic] religion and the establishment of an imperial world state."

As for the conditions under which jihad might be undertaken—when, by whom, against whom, with what sort of declaration of war, ending how, with what division of spoils, and so on these are matters that religious scholars worked out in excruciating detail over the centuries. But about the basic meaning of jihad—warfare against unbelievers to extend Muslim domains—there was perfect consensus. For example, the most important collection of hadith (reports about the sayings and actions of Muhammad), called Sahib al-Bukhari, contains 199 references to jihad, and every one of them refers to it in the sense of armed warfare against non-Muslims. To quote the 1885 Dictionary of Islam, jihad is "an incumbent religious duty, established in the Qur'an and in the traditions [hadith] as a divine institution, and enjoined especially for the purpose of advancing Islam and of repelling evil from Muslims."

Jihad was no abstract obligation through the centuries, but a key aspect of Muslim life. According to one calculation, Muhammad himself engaged in 78 battles, of which just one (the Battle of the Ditch) was defensive. Within a century after the prophet's death in 632, Muslim armies had reached as far as India in the east and Spain in the west. Though such a dramatic single expansion was never again to be repeated, important victories in subsequent centuries included the seventeen Indian campaigns of Mahmud of Ghazna (998–1030), the battle of Manzikert opening Anatolia (1071), the conquest of Constantinople (1453), and the triumphs of Uthman dan Fodio in West Africa (1804–17). In brief, jihad was part of the warp and woof not only of premodern Muslim doctrine but of premodern Muslim life.

## Variant Meanings of Jihad

That said, jihad also had two variant meanings over the ages, one of them more radical than the standard meaning and one quite pacific. The first, mainly associated with the thinker Ibn

Michael Ramirez. Reproduced by permission.

Taymiya (1268–1328), holds that born Muslims who fail to live up to the requirements of their faith are themselves to be considered unbelievers, and so legitimate targets of jihad. This tended to come in handy when (as was often the case) one Muslim ruler made war against another; only by portraying the enemy as not properly Muslim could the war be dignified as a jihad.

The second variant, usually associated with Sufis, or Muslim mystics, was the doctrine customarily translated as "greater jihad" but perhaps more usefully termed "higher jihad." This Sufi variant invokes allegorical modes of interpretation to turn jihad's literal meaning of armed conflict upside-down, calling instead for a withdrawal from the world to struggle against one's baser instincts in pursuit of numinous awareness and spiritual depth. But as Rudolph Peters notes in his authoritative *Jihad in Classical and Modern Islam* (1995), this interpretation was "hardly touched upon" in premodern legal writings on jihad.

In the vast majority of premodern cases, then, jihad signified one thing only: armed action versus non-Muslims. In modern times, things have of course become somewhat more complicated, as Islam has undergone contradictory changes resulting from its contact with Western influences. Muslims having to cope with the West have tended to adopt one of three broad approaches: Islamist, reformist, or secularist. For the purposes of this discussion, we may put aside the secularists (such as Kemal Ataturk), for they reject jihad in its entirety, and instead focus on the Islamists and reformists. Both have fastened on the variant meanings of jihad to develop their own interpretations.

## Jihad Against Impious Muslims

Islamists, besides adhering to the primary conception of jihad as armed warfare against infidels, have also adopted as their own Ibn Taymiya's call to target impious Muslims. This approach acquired increased salience through the 20th century as Islamist thinkers like Hasan al-Banna (1906–49), Sayyid Qutb (1906–66), Abu al-A'la Mawdudi (1903–79), and Ayatollah Ruhollah Khomeini (1903–89) promoted jihad against putatively Muslim rulers who failed to live up to or apply the laws of Islam. The revolutionaries who overthrew the shah of Iran in 1979 and the assassins who gunned down President Anwar Sadat of Egypt two years later overtly held to this doctrine. So does Osama bin Laden.

> *"Throughout history, the call to jihad*
> *[holy war] has rallied Muslims to the*
> *defense of Islam."*

# Islam Does Not Encourage Wars of Aggression

## John Esposito

*John Esposito argues in the following viewpoint that mainstream Islam recognizes two kinds of jihad, or holy war—the struggle against evil in one's self, or greater jihad, and the defense of Islam, or lesser jihad. Esposito claims that aggressive wars are not included in the idea of jihad. He says that extremists have hijacked the notion of jihad, misinterpreting language of the Koran to justify terrorism and other acts of aggression. He argues that Islam promotes peace, not war. Esposito, the founding director of the Centre for Muslim-Christian Understanding at Georgetown University, is the author of* Unholy War: Terror in the Name of Islam.

As you read, consider the following questions:

1. What modern day examples does the author give of the abuse of the concept of jihad?

John Esposito, "Understanding Islam," *Gulf News*, July 17, 2003. Reproduced by permission of the author.

2. According to the author, why does the Quran contain so many verses about the conduct of war?

3. What verse from the Quran does the author cite to show that Islam requires a proportional response to aggression?

Jihad (exertion or struggle) is sometimes referred to as the Sixth Pillar of Islam. The importance of jihad is rooted in the Holy Quran's command to struggle (the literal meaning of the word jihad) in the path of God and in the example of the Prophet Mohammed (PBUH)[1] and his early Companions.

The history of the Muslim community from the Prophet (PBUH) to the present day can be read within the framework of what the Holy Quran teaches about jihad. These Holy Quranic teachings have been of essential significance to Muslim self-understanding, piety, mobilisation, expansion, and defence.

Jihad as struggle pertains to the difficulty and complexity of living a good life: struggling against the evil in oneself—to be virtuous and moral, making a serious effort to do good deeds and helping to reform society.

## Types of Jihad

Depending on the circumstances in which one lives, it also can mean fighting injustice and oppression, spreading and defending Islam, and creating a just society through preaching, teaching, and, if necessary, armed struggle or holy war.

The two broad meanings of jihad, non-violent and violent, are contrasted in a well-known Prophetic tradition. It is said that when Prophet Mohammed (PBUH) returned from battle he told his followers: "We return from the lesser jihad (warfare) to the greater jihad." The greater jihad is the more

1. Peace Be Upon Him.

difficult and more important struggle against one's ego, selfishness, greed, and evil.

In its most general meaning, jihad refers to the obligation incumbent on all Muslims, individuals and the community, to follow and realise God's will: to lead a virtuous life and to extend the Islamic community through preaching, education, personal example, writing, etc.

Jihad also includes the right, indeed the obligation, to defend Islam and the community from aggression. Throughout history, the call to jihad has rallied Muslims to the defence of Islam. The Afghan mujahideen fought a decade-long jihad against Soviet occupation not long ago.

## Mainstream Versus Radical

Jihad is a concept with multiple meanings, used and abused throughout Islamic history. Although jihad has always been an important part of the Islamic tradition, in recent years some have maintained that it is a universal religious obligation for all true Muslims to join the jihad to promote Islamic reform or revolution.

Some look around them and see a world dominated by corrupt authoritarian regimes and a wealthy elite minority concerned solely with its own economic prosperity and awash in Western culture and values. Western governments are perceived as propping up oppressive regimes and exploiting the region's human and natural resources, robbing Muslims of their culture and their option to be governed according to their own choice and to live in a more just society.

Mainstream Islamic activists believe that the restoration of Muslim power and prosperity requires a return to Islam, a political or social revolution to create more Islamically oriented states or societies. A radicalised violent minority combine militancy with messianic visions to inspire and mobilise an army of God whose jihad they believe will liberate Muslims at home and abroad.

Despite the fact that jihad is not supposed to be used for aggressive warfare, it has been, and continues to be, so used by some rulers, governments, and individuals such as [former Iraqi president] Saddam Hussain in the Gulf War of 1991, the Taliban in Afghanistan, and [terrorist] Osama bin Laden and [the terrorist group] Al Qaida. . . .

## Terrorism

Historically, some Muslims have engaged in terrorism and used religion to justify their actions. For many who have little previous knowledge of Islam or Muslims, acts of terrorism committed by extremists, in particular [the September 11, 2001, terrorist attacks] raise the question of whether there is something in Islam or the Holy Quran that fosters violence and terrorism.

Islam, like all religions, neither supports nor requires illegitimate violence. The Holy Quran does not advocate or condone terrorism. The God of the Holy Quran is consistently portrayed as a God of mercy and compassion as well as a just judge.

Every verse of the Holy Quran begins with a reference to God's mercy and compassion; throughout the Holy Quran in many contexts, Muslims are reminded to be merciful and just. Indeed, whenever a pious Muslim begins an activity such as a meal, writing a letter, or driving a car, he or she says: "Al-Rahman Al-Rahim" (In the name of God the Merciful and Compassionate). However, Islam does permit, indeed at times requires, Muslims to defend themselves and their families, religion, and community from aggression.

Like all scriptures, Islamic sacred texts must be read within the social and political contexts in which they were revealed. It is not surprising that the Holy Quran, like the Hebrew scriptures or the Old Testament, has verses that address fighting and the conduct of war.

The world in which the Islamic community emerged was a rough neighbourhood. Arabia and the city of Mecca, in which Prophet Mohammed (PBUH) lived and received God's revelation, were beset by tribal raids and cycles of vengeance and vendetta. The broader Near East, in which Arabia was located, was itself divided between two warring superpowers, the Byzantine (Eastern Roman) and the Sasanian (Persian) empires.

## Defensive Jihad

The earliest Holy Quranic verses, dealing with the right to engage in a "defensive" jihad, or struggle, were revealed shortly after the hijra (emigration) of Prophet Mohammed (PBUH) and his followers to Medina in flight from their persecution in Mecca.

At a time when they were forced to fight for their lives, Prophet Mohammed (PBUH) is told: "Leave is given to those who fight because they were wronged—surely God is able to help them—who were expelled from their homes wrongfully for saying, 'Our Lord is God'" (22:39–40).

The defensive nature of jihad is clearly emphasised in 2:190: "And fight in the way of God with those who fight you, but aggress not: God loves not the aggressors." At critical points throughout the years, Prophet Mohammed (PBUH) received revelations from God that provided guidelines for the jihad.

As the Muslim community grew, questions quickly emerged as to what was proper behaviour during times of war. The Holy Quran provided detailed guidelines and regulations regarding the conduct of war: who is to fight and who is exempted (48:17, 9:91), when hostilities must cease (2:192), and how prisoners should be treated (47:4). Most important, verses such as 2:294 emphasised that warfare and the response to violence and aggression must be proportional: "Whoever transgresses against you, respond in kind."

## Islam Is Peace

The face of terror is not the true faith of Islam. That's not what Islam is all about. Islam is peace. These terrorists don't represent peace. They represent evil and war.

*George W. Bush, "Remarks by the President at Islamic Center of Washington, D.C.," September 17, 2001.*

## Peace Is the Norm

However, Holy Quranic verses also underscore that peace, not violence and warfare, is the norm. Permission to fight the enemy is balanced by a strong mandate for making peace: "If your enemy inclines towards peace, then you too should seek peace and put your trust in God" (8:61) and "Had Allah wished, He would have made them dominate you, and so if they leave you alone and do not fight you and offer you peace, then Allah allows you no way against them" (4:90).

From the earliest times, it was forbidden in Islam to kill non-combatants as well as women and children and monks and rabbis, who were given the promise of immunity unless they took part in fighting.

## Sword Verses

But what of those verses, sometimes referred to as the "sword verses," that call for killing unbelievers, such as: "When the sacred months have passed, slay the idolaters wherever you find them, and take them and confine them and lie in wait for them at every place of ambush" (9:5)?

This is one of a number of Holy Quranic verses that are cited by critics to demonstrate the inherently violent nature of Islam and its scripture. These same verses have also been selectively used (or abused) by religious extremists to develop a theology of hate and intolerance and to legitimise unconditional warfare against unbelievers.

During the period of expansion and conquest, many of the ulama (religious scholars) enjoyed royal patronage and provided a rationale for caliphs to pursue their imperial dreams and extend the boundaries of their empires.

They said that the "sword verses" abrogated or overrode the earlier Holy Quranic verses that limited jihad to defensive war: In fact, however, the full intent of "When the sacred months have passed, slay the idolaters wherever you find them" is missed or distorted when quoted in isolation. For it is followed and qualified by: "But if they repent and fulfill their devotional obligations and pay the zakat (the charitable tax on Muslims), then let them go their way, for God is forgiving and kind" (9:5).

The same is true of another often quoted verse: "Fight those who believe not in God nor the Last Day, nor hold that forbidden which hath been forbidden by God and His Apostle, nor hold the religion of truth (even if they are) of the People of the Book," which is often cited without the line that follows, "Until they pay the tax with willing submission, and feel themselves subdued" (9:29).

Throughout history, the sacred scriptures of Judaism, Christianity, and Islam have been used and abused, interpreted and misinterpreted, to justify resistance and liberation struggles, extremism and terrorism, holy and unholy wars. Terrorists like Osama bin Laden and others go beyond classical Islam's criteria for a just jihad and recognise no limits but their own, employing any weapons or means.

They reject Islamic laws regarding the goals and legitimate means for a valid jihad: that violence must be proportional and that only the necessary amount of force should be used to repel the enemy, that innocent civilians should not be targeted, and that jihad must be declared by the ruler or head of state.

Today, individuals and groups, religious and lay, seize the right to declare and legitimise unholy wars of terrorism in the name of Islam. . . .

## Violent Extremists

While the atrocities and acts of terrorism committed by violent extremists have connected Islam with terrorism, the Islamic tradition places limits on the use of violence and rejects terrorism, hijackings, and hostage taking.

As with other faiths, mainstream and normative doctrines and laws are ignored, distorted, or hijacked and misinterpreted by a radical fringe. Islamic law, drawing on the Holy Quran, sets out clear guidelines for the conduct of war and rejects acts of terrorism. Among other things, it is quite specific in calling for the protection of non-combatants as well as for proportional retaliation. . . .

Other [Quran] verses provide a strong mandate for making peace: "If your enemy inclines toward peace then you too should seek peace and put your trust in God" (8:61) and "Had Allah wished, He would have made them dominate you and so if they leave you alone and do not fight you and offer you peace, then Allah allows you no way against them" (4:90).

Since its beginnings, the Islamic community faced rebellion and civil wars, violence and terrorism, epitomised by groups like the Kharijites and Assassins. The Kharijites were a pious but puritanical and militant extremist group that broke with the caliph Ali and later assassinated him.

The Assassins lived apart in secret communities from which they were guided by a series of Grand Masters, who ruled from the mountain fortress of Alamut in northern Persia. The Assassins' jihad against the Seljuq Dynasty terrorised princes, generals, and ulama (scholars), whom they murdered in the name of the Hidden Imam. They struck such terror in the hearts of their Muslim and Crusader enemies that their exploits in Persia and Syria earned them a name and memory in history long after they were overrun and the Mongols executed their last Grand Master in 1256.

The response of Sunni Islam and Islamic law was to marginalise extremists and develop a political theory that emphasised stability over chaos and anarchy. This, of course, did not dissuade all from the extremist path.

In more recent decades, alongside mainstream Islamic political opposition, terrorist groups have risen to challenge regimes and terrorise their populations and attack foreign interests. Often they portray themselves as the "true believers" struggling against repressive regimes and in the midst of a "pagan" society of unbelief.

## Hijacking Jihad

They attempt to impose their ideological brand of Islam and "hijack" Islamic doctrines such as jihad, claiming to be defending true Islam, to legitimise their illegitimate use of violence and acts of terrorism.

In Egypt, groups like Egypt's Islamic Jihad, and other extremist groups, assassinated President Anwar Sadat and other government officials, slaughtered tourists in Luxor, burned churches and killed Christians.

In Algeria, the Armed Islamic Group has engaged in a campaign of terror against the Algerian government. Osama bin Laden and Al Qaida undertook a global war of terror against Muslim governments and America, distorting Islam and countering Islamic law in issuing their own fatwas (legal opinions) in an attempt to legitimise their war and call for attacks against civilians (noncombatants).

Although these groups tend to receive the most media coverage because of the high-profile atrocities they commit, they represent only an extremist minority, not the majority of Muslims.

| "War is never blessed by God and you cannot follow Jesus by supporting war no matter what the president wants to tell us."

# Christianity Forbids War

*John Dear*

*In this viewpoint John Dear argues that Christians must reject the just war theory, which postulates that some wars are justified. He says that Christians must return to the nonviolence taught by Christ. Early Christians, he says, were nonviolent, but Christians today have rejected Christ's teachings and have faith in weapons and government instead of God. Dear, who has been arrested seventy-five times for acts of civil disobedience, is a Jesuit priest, peace activist, and former director of the Fellowship of Reconciliation.*

As you read, consider the following questions:

1. What three nonviolent political activists does Dear cite in support of nonviolence as a way of life?
2. Quoting Ghandi, who does the author say are the only people who do not know that Jesus was nonviolent?

Stephen Morris, "Non-Violence or Non-existence: An Interview with John Dear SJ.," *Catholic New Times*, December 14, 2003. Reproduced by permission.

3. According to Dear, what is the only thing you can say about Jesus for sure?

*Catholic New Times: How do you think the early Christians would have reacted to something like a draft currently promoted by the Bush administration?*

***John Dear:*** First of all, this is to be expected. The U.S. is a blatant empire, dominating the world shamelessly, with total disregard for human life, and we're seeing that played out in Iraq. Unfortunately most people are just going right along with it, including most Christians in the U.S. But as I understand it, that's not the way it was a long, long time ago. For the first 300 years of Christianity, being a Christian meant you were not going to worship the Emperor, you were not going to join the imperial army, you refused to kill, you said that you were worshipping this guy Jesus. They immediately arrested you and they fed you to the lions. So all the early Christians were people of nonviolence, and some were martyred.

Then in 315 Constantine converted and soon after that the Just War theory began and here we are 1700 years later with Christians rejecting the Sermon on the Mount, and picking up arms.

*Why do Jesus, the early Christians and pacifists say, "It is unlawful for me to fight?"*

For one thing, I don't really use that word "pacifist." It sounds too much like the word "passive." I like that clumsy word of Gandhi and Martin Luther King, "non-violence," because in it is the phrase, "You will do no violence to anyone." But the whole point of Christianity as I understand it is that we are following Jesus and the only thing that you can say about Jesus for sure is that he was non-violent. He said we have to love one another, serve one another, be compassionate with one another, and then this—we must love our enemies. You cannot love your enemies and bomb them at the same time, or plan to kill them, or maintain 30,000 nuclear weapons to destroy the planet. Then you are no longer following Jesus. Gandhi said that Jesus was the most active practitioner of nonviolence in the history of the world and the only people who don't know that Jesus was non-violent are Christians.

You cannot support war, no matter what your government tells you, because you are following Jesus. And his last words to the community as they were dragging him away after they arrested him were: "Put down the sword!" We're not allowed to take up the sword or drop a bomb or threaten others with nuclear weapons. . . .

## No Cause Justifies Killing

*You talk about "disarming one's heart." Can you explain what you mean by that?*

I've been studying Gandhi and King and [Catholic political activist] Dorothy Day for all these years and I think that non-violence is not just a strategy or a tactic but a way of living. And it begins in the heart with a vision of a reconciled humanity, a vision that every human being is a sister or brother, that we are all children of the God of peace. We're already reconciled, already one, already united—and if you really believe that, if you enter into the spiritual vision of reality, you can never hurt or never kill another human being ever again, much less remain silent while war is waged or starvation exists and nuclear weapons are maintained. So nonviolence is this active way of love and truth that seeks justice and peace for the whole world, seeking reconciliation with everyone, deliberately resisting this systemic evil, and it operates on this one condition: there is no cause by which we would support the taking of a single human life.

I'm willing to accept suffering to undergo violence without a trace of retaliation. I'm willing to be killed, but I'm never

KILLING IN GOD'S NAME

Paul Conrad. Reproduced by permission.

ready to kill, as I pursue this vision of a unified human family. So non-violence is a whole way of life. Gandhi said it's a life-force more powerful than all the weapons of the world combined and we're just beginning to tap into it. But it begins in our heart that often, we're so used to violence, that's all we know.

I've come to the conclusion that we're all so violent that the only way to do the hard part really is with prayer and meditation, and I see this in everyone from St. Francis to Gandhi. You have to turn to the God of peace, and let God disarm our hearts so that we can become disarming people. It's a contemplative thing, a life of prayer, but it's also an active life. You have to be part of the movement.

*Some say the world is post-Christian. Some lament this but do you think the church might return to a more prophetic stance regarding war, given that Pope John Paul II totally condemned the invasion of Iraq. Are you hopeful?*

## Renounce the Just War Theory

I want it to go in that direction. I thought the whole point of the church was to follow the non-violent Jesus, which means the church is supposed to be a community of active nonviolence. The church can never support war or hold up some baloney called the Just War doctrine. It has nothing to do with Jesus. We've just gotten totally co-opted; we're part of the power structure by and large, to the point that the night before the bombing of Iraq, Billy Graham prayed with Bush in the White House and the prayer went something to the effect of: "May the bombs hit the targets and kill the enemy, in the name of our Lord Jesus." And nobody is fazed by that! They've totally missed the point of the Gospel, and are into idolatry, and blasphemy, and heresy, and this false spirituality of violence that justifies empire.

The church needs to disentangle from power and stay at the bottom with the poor, the victims and the marginalized; then it will move closer towards Jesus and the gospel. And the more it rejects war and renounces the Just War theory, the more it will turn to the Sermon on the Mount and its commandment to love our enemies, and once we start doing that, we will become prophetic people and say that war is never blessed by God and you cannot follow Jesus by supporting war no matter what the president wants to tell us.

Here in the U.S. people are numb, very comfortable and most of them are waving the flag and going to church, being very proud about the U.S. and the war in Iraq and totally oblivious to our huge arsenal of weapons of mass destruction. In effect, we are placing our security in our government and weapons and not in God.

*A reviewer of [left-wing political commentator] Michael Moore's book said that his position was basically that Americans are kind-hearted people who have been duped by an evil system. What if this is not the case? What if Americans are perfectly aware of their power and position in the world, and want to take full advantage of it. How would you respond to this? . . .*

It might be true. As I travel around the country I meet people who are by and large very good people, but gosh, we're just so comfortable that we're just clueless. I saw widespread support for the war, even among the churches, and I see wide support for our nuclear weapons and the death penalty, and anti-immigration policies, racism, and violence in general. But however we describe the situation, we're a very sick people. The phrase I use is "addicted to violence." We're so addicted we don't even know what we're doing. My hope is in the great examples of King and Dorothy Day, and the nonviolence now being discussed in the churches. I also take consolation that the peace movement in the Christian community is just beginning. We are just learning what nonviolence requires, just starting to organize for a new world without war.

> "True religion looks upon as peaceful
> those wars that are waged not for
> aggrandizement, or cruelty, but with
> the object of securing peace, of punish-
> ing evildoers, and of uplifting the
> good."

# Christianity Accepts Just Wars

*James Turner Johnson*

*James Turner Johnson describes in the following viewpoint the
origin of the just war tradition in Christianity. According to
Christian tenets, claims the author, a war is just if it is waged to
secure order, justice, and peace. He argues that wars authorized
by a sovereign government with right intention for a just cause
are permitted in Christianity. Johnson is a professor of religion
at Rutgers University, former general editor of the* Journal of
Religious Ethics, *and author of* The Holy War Idea in Western
and Islamic Traditions.

As you read, consider the following questions:

1. Who wrote, "We do not seek peace in order to be at
   war, but we go to war that we may have peace"?

James Turner Johnson, "Just War, As It Was and Is," *First Things: A Monthly Journal of
Religion and Public Life*, January 1, 2005, Copyright 2005 Institute on Religion and
Public Life. Reproduced by permission.

2. According to the author, what Biblical authority do medieval and early modern thinkers rely upon to justify the use of force?

3. What are the three prerequisites for a just war, according to St. Thomas Aquinas?

The just war tradition came into being during the Middle Ages as a way of thinking about the right use of force in the context of responsible government of the political community. With deep roots in both ancient Israel and classical Greek and Roman political thought and practice, the origins of a specifically Christian just war concept first appeared in the thought of Augustine. A systematic just war theory came only some time later, beginning with Gratian's Decretum in the middle of the twelfth century, maturing through the work of two generations of successors, the Decretists and the Decretalists, and taking theological form in the work of [Saint] Thomas Aquinas and others in the latter part of the thirteenth century. Later in the Middle Ages, and particularly during the era of the Hundred Years War, this canonical and theological conception of just war was further elaborated by incorporation of ideas, customs, and practices from the chivalric code and the experience of war, from renewed attention to Roman law, especially the *jus gentium,* and from the developing experience of government.

All this took place within a maturing theory of politics first outlined by Augustine in *City of God,* which conceived the good society as one characterized by a just order and thus one at peace both within itself and with other polities similarly justly ordered. Within this conception of politics the ruler's right to rule is defined by his responsibility to secure and protect the order and justice, and thus the peace, of his own political community and also to contribute to orderly, just, and peaceful interactions with other such communities.

## Public Authority

The place of the justified resort to force within this overall conception was, for medieval and early modern thinkers alike, encapsulated in a verse from the Apostle Paul, Romans 13:4: "For [the ruler] is God's minister to you for good. But if you do evil, be afraid; for he does not bear the sword in vain. He is God's minister, an avenger to execute wrath on him that does evil." The use of armed force in this conception was thus both strictly justified and strictly limited: it might be undertaken only on public authority and for the public good. As Aquinas summed it up in the *Summa Theologica,* for a resort to the sword to be justified it must be on the authority of a sovereign, for a just cause rightly defined, and for a right intention, which included both avoidance of evil intentions and the positive aim of securing peace—peace understood, after Augustine, as *tranquilliras ordinis,* the tranquillity of a just political order. Elsewhere in the developing tradition limits were set on how such justified force might be used: certain classes of persons were normally to be treated as noncombatants and not to be harmed directly and intentionally in their persons or property, and lists were made of weapons not to be used because of their indiscriminate or especially deadly effect.

This was the tradition of just war in its classic form. Taking explicit shape in Christian theology and canon law, it was also a Christian tradition in a broader sense—the collected consensus of the Christian culture of the West on the justified use of force, set squarely within a normative consensus on the purpose of political order. . . .

For a number of reasons Aquinas' formulation of the idea of just war provides a useful place to begin reengaging the classic just war tradition in its specifically Christian form. Let me identify three of the most important of these reasons. First, his formulation reflects and summarizes the debates of the previous century and a quarter, in which canonists and theologians collected, thought through, and systematically organized earlier normative Christian thought on the use of armed force. In particular, it exemplifies pithily and powerfully how Augustine's thought on Christian moral and political responsibility lies at the center of this developing tradition. Second, Aquinas' conception of just war was the reference point for later theorists at the beginning of the modern era. ... Third, Aquinas' conception of just war places the resort to armed force squarely in the frame of the sovereign's responsibility for the good of the public order. His three conditions necessary for a just resort to force—sovereign authority, just cause, and right intention—correspond directly to the three goods of the political community as defined in Augustinian political theory: order, justice, and peace. This conception thus provides a model for how contemporary just war thought should be set within a moral theory of good politics, both within and among societies. . . .

## Three Necessities

"For a war (*bellum*) to be just," Aquinas writes, "three things are necessary": sovereign authority, just cause, and right intention. The first thing we should note here is the concept of bellum, usually translated "war." In contemporary usage "war" has certain particular meanings which we may wrongly read back into his. In positive international law it refers to a specific relationship of conflict between or among states, and more broadly to "armed conflict" that may involve nonstate actors within states or across national borders. In the debates over humanitarian intervention in the 1990s some moralists made a distinction between "war," which they understood as having to do with state uses of armed force for their own interests, and intervention by military force for humanitarian purposes, which they regarded as altruistic and not "war." Thus in 1998 the United Presbyterian Church in the United States adopted a resolution that accepted uses of military force for humanitarian intervention only so long as there were no national interests being served; use of force for those interests was opposed. In some quarters "war" refers only to aggression by military force, to be opposed not by "war" but by "legitimate self-defense." In the post-September 11 American debate, critics have assailed the term "war on terrorism" as wrongly emphasizing military force and deemphasizing reliance on law-enforcement methods. And so on.

Bellum in medieval usage referred to any use of armed force by a sovereign ruler, whether this force was applied internally to that ruler's society or externally. Its opposite was *duellum,* use of force on private authority and thus presumptively for private purposes. Bellum, in the terms of just war theory, might be just or unjust, depending on circumstances; duellum could only be unjust. The roots of this distinction lie in Augustine's thought: the service of private ends by private persons manifests *cupiditas*—wrongly directed, self-centered love or motivation—while efforts by those at the head of communities to serve the good of those communities show the effect of a concern for justice informed by *caritas,* rightly directed love. (It is for this reason, I suggest, that Aquinas places his discussion of just war in the context of his treatment of the virtue of caritas.)

## Sovereign Authority

Only a person in a position of responsibility for the good of the entire community may rightly authorize the use of the sword. Anyone not in such a position who resorts to the sword, for reasons however lofty, is guilty of disturbing the public good. The only exception to this is the use of arms in response to an attack under way or immediately offered, but even this allowance disappears when public authority is at hand to combat this evil. So the authority of a sovereign is necessary for a just war, because we are here talking about bellum, the only kind of resort to the sword that may be just. That Aquinas puts this requirement first is not accidental but

## Force May Be Necessary

The Catechism [of the Catholic Church] presents the church's official and therefore authoritative position on all doctrinal and ethical matters. Specifically, it reaffirms, and remains in continuity with, the classic Christian position on war: namely, in a fallen world, resort to arms and coercive force may be justified, provided that certain moral criteria have been met.

*Charles J. Daryl*, Journal of Church and State, *March 22, 2005.*

follows from the logic of the concept of just war being set out: only uses of force by sovereign authority have the potential to be justified; thus this is the primary criterion. Moreover, it is an element in the sovereign's responsibility for the public good that he must weigh the cause offered to determine whether it is just and must use force so as to manifest right intention. The Neoscholastics usefully elaborated on this responsibility, including within it the sovereign's responsibility to weigh the cause and his responsibility to get advice from knowledgeable persons; yet ultimately, responsibility for the decision about whether to use force rests with the sovereign alone.

## Just Cause

In listing the just causes for war Aquinas named two, citing them by means of a quotation from Augustine: recovery of that which has been wrongly taken, and punishment of evil. Not explicitly named here is the sole just cause for a state's resort to force on its own authority that is clearly allowed in our contemporary positive international law: self-defense against an attack under way or clearly imminent. The canon law from Gratian onward had included such defense in its listing of just causes for resort to arms, citing Isidore of Seville as the source. Aquinas surely knew the canonists on just war, so his omission of one of the three just causes recognized by the canon law needs some explanation. Keeping in mind the importance of Romans 13:4, Alfred Vanderpol has argued that for Thomas, and Scholastic just war theory in general, punishment of evil was the overarching just cause for resort to armed force, so that defense against attack was included within this category. This is, I think, close to the mark, but I suggest that Vanderpol has the relation reversed. Within the logic of Aquinas' just war theory, defense of the common good—protecting just order and therefore peace—is the central rationale for just war as a whole. Punishment of evil and retaking that which has been wrongly taken are thus two specific justifying causes within this larger conception of defense of the common good.

That Aquinas does not follow the canonists in explicitly naming defense against attack as a just cause for resort to force follows, I suggest, from his commitment to this larger conception of defense. Of course, the sovereign has the right to authorize resort to the sword in defense against attack under way or immediately offered; even private persons have such a right. But Aquinas does not build up a conception of defense as just cause on the basis of the private right of self-defense; rather, he builds down from his overall conception of the sovereign's responsibility for the good of the political community. Insofar as the need for defense provides just cause for public use of the sword, it comes from the responsibility of government to protect order, justice, and peace, not simply from the right to respond to an attacker in kind.

For a variety of reasons, including most importantly the change in the idea of sovereignty to the Westphalian model of a nation-state's territorial integrity, the development of international law on the state's right to use force has proceeded in the opposite direction, focusing on the right of self-defense. Recovery of that which has been wrongly taken and punishment of evildoing are not explicitly named as justifications for the use of armed force by states in international law, but arguably they have been subsumed into the concept of self-defense: the former being recast as defense against an armed attack still in progress, as in the recovery of Kuwait from Iraq in 1991, the latter being recast as the right of retaliation. In any case, we see that there are some significant differences between the idea of just cause in the classic just war tradition and contemporary international law. It may be that moral reflection on the former provides a useful critical perspective on the latter.

## Right Intention

The third necessity Aquinas names for a just resort to arms is right intention. If one reads recent Catholic just war thinking one regularly finds the idea of right intention collapsed into just cause or used to reinforce that moral requirement, as in this formulation from the Catholic bishops of the United States: "Force may be used only for a truly just cause and solely for that purpose." For Aquinas the requirement of right intention is much more than this. He treats this requirement in two ways, negatively and positively. Negatively, he rules out evil intentions, exemplified in Augustine's list from Contra Fausturn: "What is evil in war? It is not the deaths of some who will soon die anyway. The desire for harming, the cruelty of avenging, an unruly and implacable animosity, the rage of rebellion, the lust of domination and the like—these are the things which are to be blamed in war." Positively, right intention is the purpose of establishing or restoring a disordered peace, or as Augustine puts it: "We do not seek peace in order to be at war, but we go to war that we may have peace." Both the positive and the negative aspects of right intention are included in this third quotation, which Aquinas draws from the canon law (but wrongly ascribes to Augustine): "True

91

religion looks upon as peaceful those wars that are waged not for aggrandizement, or cruelty, but with the object of securing peace, of punishing evildoers, and of uplifting the good."

Right intention, then, as defined by Aquinas, includes both the avoidance of wrong intention and the positive aim of securing peace. It does not simply reduce to a restatement or reinforcement of the requirement of just cause. Rather, it focuses on two other things: the state of mind of the one who authorizes the war and those who fight under that authorization, and the fundamental moral purpose for all uses of force—to achieve the peace that comes only with a justly ordered community. So once again, his conception of just war takes us back to the conception of politics within which—and only within which—the resort to armed force may be both justified and necessary. This is the full meaning of just war according to Aquinas.

> *"From a Buddhist point of view, anger and violence have to be met with the opposite, compassion. By meeting anger with anger, one adds fuel to the fire."*

# Buddhism Forbids War

*Mahinda Deegalle*

*Buddhist Sri Lanka is experiencing political violence between two ethnic groups, the Sinhala and Tamil. Some Sinhalese claim that such violence is not forbidden by Buddhism while others disagree. In the following viewpoint Mahinda Deegalle argues that Buddha's teachings, Buddha's own life, and the writings of Buddhist scholars prove that Buddhism can never be used to justify violence, no matter what the circumstance. Deegalle is a Buddhist monk from Sri Lanka and a lecturer in the study of religions at Bath Spa University College in the United Kingdom.*

As you read, consider the following questions:

1. How does the author define "emic" and "etic?"

2. What type of action do Buddhists believe is the only action that will in the long run create a stable and

Mahinda Deegalle, "Is Violence Justified in Theravada Buddhism?," *The Ecumenical Review*, April 1, 2003. Copyright 2003 World Council of Churches. Reproduced by permission.

peaceful environment, according to Deegalle?

3. According to the author, what does Buddhism believe is more important than any material thing or ideology?

Is there a place for violence in Theravada Buddhism? This question is often raised when various recent events are examined in relation to the ethnic conflict in Sri Lanka and the genocide of 2–3 million Khmers (mostly Buddhists) between 1975 and 1979 by Pol Pot and the Khmer Rouge in Cambodia. Both Sri Lanka and Cambodia are primarily Theravada Buddhist societies and in the last three decades both countries have witnessed a great deal of physical violence and abuse of human rights. . . .

## Nonviolence Is Consensus

The overwhelming consensus among the scholars of Buddhism is that Buddhism is against violence. This scholarly consensus is neither a confessional view nor an exaggeration of the real situation. The pacifist image of Buddhist teachings and historical practices of non-violent actions in Buddhist communities are very much supported by and grounded on Pali canonical scriptures.[1]

Presenting an emic (emic = an attempt to understand the viewpoint of the people themselves, as opposed to etic which is the viewpoint of the observer) view of the pacifist image of Buddhism, Walpola Rahula, the renowned Buddhist scholar monk of Sri Lanka, articulated well the Buddhist non-violent perspective in one of his early popular writings:

> This spirit of tolerance and understanding has been from the beginning one of the most cherished ideals of Buddhist culture and civilization. That is why there is not a single example of persecution or the shedding of a drop of blood in converting people to Buddhism, or in its propagation

---

1. The Pali Canon is a collection of early Buddhist writings important to Buddhism.

during its long history of 2500 years. It spread peacefully all over the continent of Asia, having more than 500 million adherents today. Violence in any form, under any pretext whatsoever, is absolutely against the teachings of the Buddha.

Thus Rahula clearly reiterated that violence has no place within Buddhist teachings or cultural practices in Buddhist communities. He highlighted that in the expansion of Buddhism from India to Sri Lanka, Burma, Thailand, China, Korea, Japan, Tibet and Central Asia, Buddhist monks and nuns embraced the principles of "tolerance" towards pre-Buddhist religious practices and beliefs while injecting intellectual and spiritual resources to enrich and nourish whatever culture, civilization or ethnic group they encountered.

Buddhist teachings maintain that under any circumstance, whether political, religious, cultural or ethnic, violence cannot be accepted or advocated to solve disputes between nations. All Buddhist traditions unanimously agree that war cannot be the solution to disputes and conflicts either. Even to achieve a religious goal, violence cannot be used and justified. A Buddhist cannot imagine a principle of "just war". How can a "war" be a "just" one? How can the slaughter of human beings be justified as "morally right"? As Premasiri has convincingly asserted by examining the early Buddhist standpoint, even in the case of solving social conflicts such as war Buddhism "does not advocate violence under any circumstance". When "insider" perspectives are examined across Buddhist cultures and combined with doctrinal understandings, one can comprehend the Buddhist abhorrence of violence and desire to seek creative strategies for a non-violent path in overcoming violence. . . .

## Loving-Kindness

Several narratives in the Pali Canon illustrate that Buddha's disciples adhered to the Buddha's teaching of loving-kindness. The story of Venerable Punna, for example, relates that he desired to live in a remote province called Sunaparanta which was notorious for cruelty and violence. When the Buddha asked Punna how he would respond if the residents there reviled, abused and assaulted him, he replied that he would not show anger and ill will towards them:

"Punna, the people of Sunaparanta are fierce . . . If the people of Sunaparanta revile . . ., how will it be for you there, Punna?" "If the people of Sunaparanta revile and abuse me . . . I will say, 'Goodly indeed are these people of Sunaparanta . . . in that they do not strike me a blow with their hands' . . . If the people of Sunaparanta deprive me of life with a sharp knife . . . I will say, 'There are disciples . . . disgusted by the body . . . look about for a knife . . . I have come upon this very knife without having looked about for it.'"

This narrative alone clearly demonstrates the tolerant attitude towards violence of an early disciple of the Buddha. What attracts one most is Punna's deep commitment to non-violence and his practice of patience even if he risks losing his own life.

The Buddhist attitude towards violence stands out as an extreme non-violent position: a path leading to total abstention from engaging in violent activities. Even in cases of extreme aggression and violence, Buddhism seems to advocate moral restraint and kindness towards those who commit crimes. This is because of the belief that only action based on loving-kindness (metta) will in the long run generate a stable and peaceful environment.

Several canonical and non-canonical sources elaborate the appreciation of a nonviolent path. One of the Jataka narratives, for instance, illustrates the Buddhist standpoint towards violence and non-violence. It discusses the policies of two kings and their strategies in overcoming violence and other social problems. One king has a reactionary approach in which "he meets force with force, mildness with mildness, he wins over the good with good and conquers the evil with evil". The

## War Can Never Be Excused

In all His teachings the Buddha stresses how sacred and precious life, especially human life is. He has said "A single day of life is worth more than all the treasures of the universe" (the Saddharma Pundharika Sutra or the 'Lotus Sutra'). War, which cruelly robs people, can never be excused by any reason or cause. It is an absolute evil. Those who advocate war or terrorism, are in fact cowards.

*Ru Wickremasinghe,* Lanka Daily News, *September 3, 2002.*

other king has a completely different strategy of a pacifist nature. In responding to social conflicts and other problems, rather than repeating violent actions he "conquers wrath with kindness, evil with good, greed with charity and falsehood with truth". His state policy seems to be based on the principles proposed in the following Dhammapada verse 223:

Hatred should be conquered by non-hatred. Unrighteousness should be conquered by righteousness. Miserliness should be conquered by generosity. A person who speaks untruth should be conquered by truth.

This latter king's approach represents a Buddhist approach and a Buddhist solution to overcoming unhealthy social problems; its strength is love, kindness, charity, truth and forbearance. It is a virtuous approach, overcoming violence through a path of non-violence. Because of the healthy aspect of the approach, the state policy of the latter king is considered superior to that of the former. This appreciation is based on the fundamental conviction that only a non-violent path will generate a long-lasting solution to any violent situation.

## Buddha's Example

During his life-time, the Buddha himself faced both verbal and physical violence. As the Pali Canon records, some had verbally abused him; others, like his cousin Devadatta, had even physically abused the Buddha, attempting to kill him. This is not the whole story of the Buddha's encounter with violence during his teaching career. In his own life, there were a few rare cases in which he himself had to intervene, for instance when some of his relatives waged war against each other over a petty dispute about water. After considerable deliberation, the Buddha himself once intervened in the war between the Sakyas and Koliyas over a dispute concerning the use of water taken from River Rohini. In that context, the Buddha pointed out that human life is worthier than what they were fighting for. It was the Buddha's fundamental conviction that human life is intrinsically more valuable than any other material or ideological thing. From the textual sources of the Pali Canon, it is clear that an appropriate method of conflict resolution is possible only through the reconciliation of the parties involved.

According to Buddhist teachings, a viable solution to conflict is less likely through the use of violent means. This is because of the belief in Buddhist doctrine that violence breeds hatred. Thus victory achieved through violence is not a permanent solution to any conflict. As the Samyutta Nikaya puts it, "Victory arouses enmity and the defeated live in sorrow." By causing pain to others, one cannot achieve happiness: one always has to think how one's actions affect others. The Dhammapada verse 131 asserts that one's own happiness comes with the happiness of others:

> Whoever, seeking one's own happiness, harms with a rod other pleasure-loving beings, experiences no happiness hereafter.

The most outstanding and famous Buddhist pacifist attitude is found in the Dhammapada verse 5: "Hatred is never ceased by hatred in this world." From a Buddhist point of view, reconciliatory methods of conflict resolution are more effective than coercive methods. As Buddhists, we are more encouraged to seek peaceful solutions to any conflict by abandoning force, intimidation and threats. In the short run, those who are involved in violent activities in the hope of liberating the masses may think that violent means can be very effective. However, in the long run, only a peaceful solution will bring harmony to society at large.

## Rage is Quelled by Compassion

This pacifist standpoint of the Dhammapada was elaborated and extended in the 13th-century Sinhala prose text, Dharmasena Thera's Saddharmaratnavaliya ("The Jewel Garland of the Good Doctrine"). Since this late medieval text is useful in understanding the Sinhala world-view, let us look at the Saddharmaratnavaliya's positions towards hatred and its reaffirmation of the power of loving-kindness and compassion. The narrative of the Demoness Kali illustrates the Theravada attitude towards violence, and maintains the early Buddhist pacifist doctrine without recommending violence and completely ignoring the controversial position of the Pali Chronicles. The Saddharmaratnavaliya states that hatred can be overcome only with compassion. This important narrative begins with a cliche:

> As a bush fire burning out of control stops only when it reaches a vast body of water, so the rage of one who vows vengeance cannot be quelled except by the waters of compassion.

Thus from a Buddhist point of view, anger and violence have to be met with the opposite, compassion. By meeting anger with anger, one adds fuel to the fire. This crucial message is clearly expressed to a Buddhist audience in very simple language. Its moral position is: "Vengeance is an extremely vile sin. Therefore, give it up." Following the canonical standpoint, it also reiterates that one cannot overcome violence through violence:

> When your body is filthy with spit . . . you cannot clean it with same spit. . . . So when you abuse those who abuse and revile you, kill or beat up those murderers who beat you . . . it is like adding fuel to fire; enmity on both sides never ceases . . . hatred that burns on the fuel of justifications must be quenched with the water of compassion, not fed with the firewood of reasons and causes. Compassion is fundamentally right, free of malice, and is the source for all good actions. Good, founded on compassion, destroys evil and puts out the fire of enmity.

This single narrative in the Saddharmaratnavaliya clearly states the Buddhist position towards violence. Violence, no matter in what form it is manifested, has to be met with non-violent measures. Solutions to conflict should be found only through non-violent means. Violence cannot solve problems. Only non-violence brings peace.

> *"Spreading the [Buddhist] religion constitutes just cause for war; it constitutes sacrificing one moral obligation for another."*

# Buddhism Permits Defensive Wars

*Tessa Bartholomeusz*

*In this viewpoint Tessa Bartholomeusz contends that many Buddhists in Sri Lanka rightly defend the use of violence to defend Buddhism. Bartholomeusz argues that the use of war to spread or defend Buddhism is supported by a reading of the history of Buddhism in Sri Lanka and by many Buddhist monks. Bartholomeusz is a professor in the Department of Religion at Florida State University and author of* In Defense of Dharma: Just-War Ideology in Buddhist Sri Lanka.

As you read, consider the following questions:

1. What Sri Lankan Buddhist king united Sri Lanka by force, according to stories cited by the author?
2. How many Buddhist monks did the author interview for her study?

Tessa Bartholomeusz, "In Defense of Dharma: Just-War Ideology in Buddhist Sri Lanka," *Journal of Buddhist Ethics*, vol. 10, 2003. Reproduced by permission.

3. What ethnicity is predominant in Sri Lanka's government, as related by Bartholomeusz?

[W]hile there is a narrative thread in Sri Lankan Buddhist history and in contemporary rhetoric that
endorses pacifism, there are Buddhist stories that argue that,
for the defense of Buddhism—that is, of the Dharma—
violence and war are permissible, even necessary, under certain
conditions. In other words, this study will probe a type of
Buddhist "just-war thinking" that calls into question scholarly
obedience to the canon's narratives of pacifism. Moreover,
inasmuch as the data suggest that Sri Lankan Buddhists have
taken (and take) full advantage of the range of resources
available to them to legitimate their ethical stance on war—
namely, canonical and post-canonical stories, this study aims
to demonstrate that inquiry into the full heritage of Sinhala-
Buddhist ethics should not be limited to a survey of the Pali
canon. . . .

## Buddhist War

Before we refer to the stories that provide justifications for
war, it is important to note that many of the (approximately
fifty) monks and laity that I interviewed for this study are well
known in Sri Lanka as proponents of "finishing the war," that
is, of eradicating the Liberation Tigers of Tamil Eelam (LTTE)
who, since 1983, have been unabashed in their claims for a
"homeland" in the north of the island. In other words, the
high profile of the Buddhist defenders of the government's
resort to war—in and of itself—supports the premise of this
essay—namely, that Buddhists have and do justify war. And
while the war that has ensued as a result of territorial claims
has no readily identifiable religious component, Buddhist
monks and laity alike justify—with Buddhist rhetoric—the
predominately Sinhala and predominately Buddhist
government's use of deadly force to quash the LTTE. As we

shall see, proponents of the war—who couch their justifications in Buddhist rhetoric—argue that preservation of the integrity of Sri Lanka is tantamount to "just cause" for war. It must also be stressed, however, that those who make arguments for war—based on their interpretation of Buddhism—also maintain that Buddhism demands compassion and non-violence. How to balance the demands of non-violence with the protection of the entire island of Sri Lanka as a Buddhist territory has remained a constant feature of political and religious rhetoric in Sri Lanka since at least the 1890s, when archival resources allow for a comprehensive view.

In the 1990s, of course, with an actual war raging in the north of Sri Lanka, the discussion about war has moved from the realm of the theoretical to the reality of the deaths, since 1983, of thousands upon thousands of Tamils and Sinhalas. Which has, to say the least, issued forth many responses, some of which condemn the war, others of which support it. No matter the position, it is generally supported by Buddhist stories. Indeed, in one of my interviews conducted in 1998, the Venerable Athuraliya Rathana, who is the coordinating secretary of the National Sangha Council, alleged that there are many stories in the canon that depict the Buddha as an advocate of force and violence if there is just cause. Some of these stories are about the Buddha; others are told by him. The Venerable Rathana cited, among others, the *Cakkavatti Sihanada Sutta*, which depicts a king, committed to the Dharma, who is flanked by a four-fold army nonetheless. For the monk, these images suggest that even the Buddha, who taught that the paradigmatic Buddhist king is a pacifist, realized that war is a reality of life and that, for defensive measures, war can be justified. For the monk, the *Cakkavatti Sihanada Sutta* provides the contemporary Sri Lankan government (which is predominately Sinhala and Buddhist) with the Buddhist justification it needs to proceed with the war against the LTTE. A Buddhist layman, the outspoken and controversial Nalin de Silva, suggested that the reason that the king could be righteous and teach pacifism in the first place had to do with his having an army: "only after non-Buddhists saw his army could he pacify them and bring them to Buddhism." Thus, for de Silva, the army in the sutta is a vehicle for forcing people—through subtle manipulation—to convert to the Dharma. Moreover, in de Silva's line of thinking, the presence of the army indicates that even a righteous Buddhist king might have to fight a defensive war to protect Buddhism.

In addition to canonical stories, post-canonical narratives have been used by Sri Lankan Buddhists to justify violence, even war. For example, a monk, writing in 1957 to the newspaper, the *Bauddha Peramuna*—a forum for Buddhist monks to air their grievances—employed a post-canonical Buddhist story of war to legitimate the appropriate use of violence. In fact, the monk was provoked by what he considered to be misuse of a Sri Lankan Buddhist story: he took exception to an allusion of Buddhism and war in a local paper that aligned the then prime minister, SWRD Bandaranaike, with Dutugemunu, the Buddhist hero of the fifth-century, post-canonical *Mahavamsa*. In his editorial, the monk asks Bandaranaike "to read the Mahavamsa," the text that chronicles the history of Buddhism in Sri Lanka, and to heed its lessons:

> Dutugemunu conquered by the sword and united the land [Sri Lanka] without dividing it among our enemies [i.e., the Tamils] and established Sinhala and Buddhism as the state language and religion.

In his allusion to the great Buddhist king Dutugemunu—who, according to the *Mahavamsa*, interrupted "*damila*" suzerainty over Anuradhapura, an ancient northern kingdom of the island—the monk correspondent of the *Bauddha Peramuna* justified violence against the Tamil minority who, for him, constituted the island's "enemies," just as they did (from the monk's point of view) in Dutugemunu's day. (It is important

---

## Pacifism Can Only Go So Far

In the midday quiet of a monastery prayer room [in Sri Lanka], where only the rattle of a ceiling fan disturbs the stillness, a Buddhist monk insists he wants peace for his country.

But pacifism, says Athuraliye Rathana, can only go so far.

"You try to kill me, and I safeguard myself," Rathana said, his yellow robe ruffling as he waved his hands. "We always hope for a peaceful society, but we know it can't be built just on words."

*Tim Sullivan, "Sri Lanka's influential Buddhist monks talk battle, not harmony," AP Worldstream, November 14, 2003.*

---

to note that, whatever the *Mahavamsa*'s meaning of the Pali word *damila*, the Sinhala word for Tamil is *demala*, while twentieth-century Sinhala interpreters of Dutugemunu's war against *damilas* translate *damila* as Tamil, *demala*). . . .

Sinhalas maintain that they are the Buddha's chosen people, and that the island of Sri Lanka is the Buddhist promised land. . . .

## Sacred Island

[Some Sinhalas believe that] Sri Lanka is a sacred island because the Buddha, by word and by deed, declared it to be so: according to the *Mahavamsa*, the Buddha made three magical trips to Sri Lanka, each time colonizing another area of the island, in preparation for the formal introduction of Buddhism two centuries after his death. Thus, Perera's view—based on readings of the *Mahavamsa*—that the entire island is the sacred home of the Sinhalas *and* of Buddhism and, therefore, is not to be divided. Philosophy of Perera's ilk has been elucidated by H.L. Seneviratne, who has argued persuasively that the *Mahavamsa*'s story of the establishment of Buddhism in Sri Lanka, in which the "island of Sri Lanka and its inhabitants, as the guardians of Buddhism, are placed under divine protection," continues to resonate in the present.

## Buddha Used Force

In his analysis of the *Mahavamsa* story regarding the establishment of Buddhism in Sri Lanka, R.A.L.H. Gunawardana has argued that there is dissonance between the Buddha of *Mahavamsa* and the Buddha of the Pali canon, the latter of which provides the textual foundation of Sri Lankan Buddhism (and Theravada Buddhism, generally). In that study, Gunawardana maintains that the *Mahavamsa* story about the Buddha's alleged first visit to the island, in which he rids Sri Lanka of forces inimical to Buddhism, provides the warrant for the use of violence for the sake of Buddhism.

According to Gunawardana's reading of the *Mahavamsa*, the Buddha's expulsion of the *yakkhas*—the non-human inhabitants of the island—contrasts with descriptions in the Pali canon of the Buddha taming similar creatures. In reinforcing the distinction, Gunawardana argues that while in the canon the Buddha uses compassion to convince non-believers of his Dharma, in the *Mahavamsa*, the Buddha uses force; in his "taming" of the *yakkhas*, the Buddha who, in the story, is referred to as the "Conqueror" (*Jina*), imposes "devious afflictions" upon the non-believers, driving them from their homeland. . . .

## Criteria for War

According to some of the Buddhists I interviewed in the summers of 1997 and 1998, Dutugemunu's saga provides contemporary Buddhists with the criteria to argue for just war (*dharma yuddhava*); the saga reminds them of the prospect that they can be faced with conflicting obligations—namely, the obligation of non-violence and the duty to protect the Dharma, which might call for violence. Put differently, according to my informants' reading, the *Mahavamsa*'s rendering of ethical duties is based on prima facie responsibilities rather than on absolute duties. In other words, the duty of non-violence can be overridden—though the justification to do so is extremely weighty—if certain criteria are met. In the *Mahavamsa*, just-war thinking provides a scenario in which Dutugemunu's violent actions are justified and in which non-violence—rendered palpable by Dutugemunu's guilt—remains the guiding force.

The reading that Dutugemunu's duty of non-violence has been overridden by his duty to establish Buddhism further throughout the island is plausible in light of the exchange between the *arahants* and the troubled king. With their power to read the king's mind, they discern his profound discomfort for having taken life (that is, the lives of King Elara with sixty thousand men), and eight of them travel to his side to console him. He asks them how he will ever find comfort, considering what he had done, that he had killed such a lot of people. The *arahants* respond with their own just-war thinking:

> Only one and a half human beings have been slain here by thee, O lord of men. The one had come unto the (three) refuges, the other had taken unto himself the five precepts. Unbelievers and men of evil life were the rest, not more to be esteemed than beasts. But as for thee, thou wilt bring glory to the doctrine of the Buddha in manifold ways; therefore cast away care from the heart, O ruler of men (xxv. 108–112).

In other words, the enlightened beings counsel Dutugemunu with their criteria for assessing his war with the damila king, which includes Dutugemunu's sacrifice of his obligation as a Buddhist not to take life. For the *arahants*, spreading the religion constitutes just cause for war; it constitutes sacrificing one moral obligation for another.

# Periodical Bibliography

The following articles have been selected to supplement the diverse views in this chapter:

Rob Asghar        "Is Faith an Impediment to Peace? Religion Doesn't Kill People, People Kill People," *Los Angeles Daily News*, October 10, 2004.

Bill Broadway     "TV Debate Delineates Christian Divide on War: Mainline Churches Against, Evangelicals For," *Washington Post*, March 15, 2003.

Richard Dawkins   "Is God the Root of All Evil?" *Independent* (London), January 6, 2006.

Derek H. Davis    "Respecting Religious Differences: The Missing Ingredient in Creating a Peaceful World Order," *Journal of Church and State*, March 22, 2005.

Paul Marshall     "Hinduism and Terror," *First Things*, June 1, 2004.

Martin E. Marty   "Religious Strangers as Menaces," *Cross Currents*, March 22, 2005.

Jackie Mason and  "Islam Is a Religion of What?" *Jewish World
Raoul Felder      Review*, July 7, 2004.

Michael McAteer   "Interfaith Peace Summit: Women Take Larger Role in Peacemaking in Africa," *Catholic New Times*, April 10, 2005.

David Smock       "Divine Intervention: Regional Reconciliation Through Faith," *Harvard International Review*, January 1, 2004.

CHAPTER 3

# Are Religion and Science in Conflict?

# Chapter Preface

Both religion and science are ways of explaining the world. Science utilizes the scientific method, which involves making observations, creating hypotheses based upon the observations, using the hypotheses to make predictions, and testing the predictions by experiment or further observation. By this method scientists create theories that explain natural phenomena. Religious explanations of the world are based upon divine revelations, holy writings, and faith. Through these, people learn how and why the world was created. Although many people see science and religion at odds, others see them as compatible. In fact, numerous scientists throughout the ages have claimed that their understanding of the world was informed by both science and religion.

During the sixteenth century, for example, astronomer Nicolaus Copernicus postulated that Earth revolves around the Sun, contradicting Church teachings, which claimed that Earth was the center of the universe. His writings were condemned by the Church as heretical. In 1633 Italian scientist Galileo Galilei faced trial before the Inquisition and was forced to renounce his belief in Copernicus's theories. He was spared capital punishment because he recanted, but he spent the remainder of his life under house arrest. Notably, Galileo did not believe science conflicted with religion, saying "I do not feel obliged to believe that the same God who has endowed us with sense, reason, and intellect has intended us to forego their use." Nearly three centuries later, Albert Einstein echoed Galileo's words:

> Everyone who is seriously involved in the pursuit of science becomes convinced that a spirit is manifest in the laws of the universe—a spirit vastly superior to that of man, and one in the face of which we with our modest powers must feel humble. In this way the pursuit of science leads to a

religious feeling of a special sort, which is indeed quite different from the religiosity of someone more naive.

Many scientists today echo those same sentiments. A 2005 survey of scientists at elite research universities found that two-thirds believe in God. In a separate study that same year, 76 percent of doctors surveyed said they believed in God, and 59 percent believed in some sort of afterlife.

Nonscientists do not necessarily share this comfortable acceptance of both scientific findings and religious beliefs. Many adherents believe literally in religious teachings and find scientific findings a threat to their beliefs. Einstein tried to explain the reason for this:

> It is [the] mythical, or rather, symbolic, content of the religious traditions which is likely to come into conflict with science. This occurs whenever this religious stock of ideas contains dogmatically fixed statements on subjects which belong in the domain of science. Thus, it is of vital importance for the preservation of true religion that such conflicts be avoided when they arise from subjects which, in fact, are not really essential for the pursuance of the religious aims.

To many believers, of course, these stories are not myths or symbols, but are facts that are essential to religious faith. Over 60 percent of Americans polled in 2004 said they believed that the biblical accounts of a six-day creation, Noah's ark, and Moses's parting of the Red Sea for the Israelites were literally true.

It may seem surprising that individuals who know the most about science are often the least troubled by its possible threat to religion. Possibly, the more scientists learn about the world, the more they realize how little they know, which evokes a sense of awe and humility, an openness to religious explanations. Other people of faith, however, believe that the teachings of science undermine religious faith. In this chapter, the authors explore whether science and religion are in conflict.

> "Because these structures exhibit complex-specified information, a quality known only to be produced by intelligent agents, we conclude that these irreducibly complex structures are intelligently designed."

# Intelligent Design Is a Scientific Theory

**Intelligent Design and Evolution Awareness Center**

*The Intelligent Design and Evolution Awareness (IDEA) Center is an organization dedicated to promoting intelligent design on its scientific merits. In this viewpoint, IDEA argues that complex biological structures, such as microbiological machines, are best explained by an intelligent cause because they have the same machinelike structural and informational properties found in things commonly known to be designed by intelligent agents. Much of the complexity observed in the natural world, says IDEA, is best explained by the action of intelligence.*

As you read, consider the following questions:

1. Does intelligent design, as described in this viewpoint, depend upon the idea of God?

Intelligent Design and Evolution Awareness Center, "The Science of IDEA," *www.idea-center.org, 2006.* © 2006 IDEA Center. Reproduced by permission.

2. The explanatory power of evolution theory is, according to IDEA, limited primarily to what type of processes?

Intelligent design is a scientific theory which says that some aspects of nature are best explained by an intelligent cause. Intelligent design begins with observations about how intelligent agents act when they design things. In short, intelligent design theory makes inferences based upon observations about the types of complexity that are produced by the action of intelligent agents.

## Observing the Natural World

Intelligent design begins with observations about the types of information that we observe being produced by intelligent agents in the real world. Even the atheist zoologist Richard Dawkins says that intuitively, "[b]iology is the study of complicated things that give the appearance of having been designed for a purpose." Dawkins would say that natural selection is what actually did the "designing," however intelligent design theorist Stephen C. Meyer rightly notes that, "[i]ndeed, in all cases where we know the causal origin of 'high information content,' experience has shown that intelligent design played a causal role." Thus, like any true scientific theory, intelligent design theory begins with empirical observations from the natural world.

When intelligent agents act, they tend to produce high levels of "complex-specified information" (CSI) and in our experience, complex-specified information is always the product of the action of intelligent design. From observing intelligent agents in the natural world, we know how to produce machines containing high levels of complex and specified information. CSI is a mathematical concept employed by William Dembski, philosopher/mathematician. In our experience, CSI is always the product of ID. The origin of CSI cannot be explained by any naturalistic process, such as evolution.

To better understand complex specified information, consider this analogy: If you saw a mountainside in South Dakota bearing a striking resemblance to four famous presidents, you would not be tempted to comment "Look what the wind and rain did!" It would be clear that the likenesses arose by design, even though you did not see the design occur, and know nobody claiming to be the sculptor. We intuitively recognize the mountainside was designed because it contains complex information (the shape of the mountainside) that conforms to specific pattern (the likeness of the presidents).

## Complexity Suggests a Designer

When we look at biology, very complex machine-like entities exist, which must be exactly as they are, or they cease to function properly. They have CSI because they are specified in that they conform to a particular pattern of arrangement organization which is necessary for them to function, and complex because they have an unlikely arrangement of many interacting parts.

The high level of complex-specified information in these biological machines makes them "irreducibly complex": they have many interacting parts (making them complex) which must be EXACTLY as they are in order for the machine to work properly (making them specified). In irreducible complexity, any change in the nature or arrangement of these parts would destroy their function and make the machine stop working. They are irreducibly complex in that they could not be any less complex and still function. Importantly, irreducibly complex structures cannot be built up through a Darwinian evolutionary process, because Darwinian evolution says that a biological structure must be functional along every small-step of its evolution, and "reverse engineering" of these structures shows that they cease to function if changed even slightly.

Because these structures exhibit complex-specified information, a quality known only to be produced by intelligent design, we conclude that these irreducibly complex structures are intelligently designed. There is also no known natural mechanism to explain the origin of these "irreducibly complex" biological structures, firming up the inference to design.

In all of this, there have been no mentions of God, religion, or adherence to any religious text but rather intelligent design is seen to rely solely upon observations about how intelligent design works in the present to look at aspects of the natural world to see if they were designed. Intelligent design theory is based solely upon applying observations about intelligent action and principles of information theory to the construction of biological systems, and nothing more. There is nothing mystical, supernatural, religious, or non-scientific about intelligent design theory. Intelligent design theory makes no statements beyond which are possible to make using inferences from the available observations of the natural world. The IDEA Center believes that intelligent design is a potent and compelling scientific theory which can explain the origin of much of life on Earth.

For more information about intelligent design theory please see:

- Intelligent Design Theory in a Nutshell
- The Science Behind Intelligent Design
- Introduction to Intelligent Design
- Intelligent Design Jargon Explained
- Evidence for Design of the Universe through Anthropic Principles

## Americans Weigh in on Intelligent Design

A Harris poll conducted in June 2005 asked Americans the question, "Which of the following do you believe about how human beings came to be?"

| | |
|---|---|
| Human beings evolved from earlier species. | 22% |
| Human beings were created directly by God. | 64% |
| Human beings are so complex that they required a powerful force or intelligent being to help create them. | 10% |
| Not sure/Decline to answer | 4% |

*The Harris Poll #52, July 6, 2005. www.harrisinteractive.com.*

## Deficiencies in Naturalistic Explanations of Life's Origins

The IDEA Center believes that there are many problems with naturalistic explanations for the origin and diversification of life. Naturalistic explanations are those which assume that there were no forces involved in the history of life other than matter, energy, and the chemical and physical laws governing their interactions. Naturalistic explanations assume that there were no intelligent agents which could have influenced life in the past.

To explain very briefly, problems in naturalistic explanations go down to the very beginning of the universe. There is no explanation for the "fine-tuning" of the physical laws of universe which allows life to exist and flourish on Earth. Models for the natural chemical origin of life face major evidential problems, such as how a "primordial soup" might have formed, or how the irreducible complexity of the simplest cell could arise.

Once life does form, the fossil record indicates that biological complexity typically appears with a "bang" and that rapid increases in biological diversity stretch Darwin's theory of evolution beyond what can be accounted for through naturalistic mechanisms of evolutionary change. Furthermore, there appear to be few plausible examples of transitional forms in the fossil record, a major line of evidence counting against naturalistic evolutionary transitions in the history of life.

Many lines of evidence that supposedly support a natural evolutionary history seem to be deficient. Methods of producing evolutionary family trees or "phylogenies" provide weak evidence for common descent as comparisons of different characteristics commonly lead to conflicting trees. Developmental biology is forced to resort to extreme examples of convergent evolution as supposedly analogous body parts are produced by the same genes in different organisms! Similarly many supposedly "homologous" organs are produced via different developmental pathways, bringing into question claims of evidence for common ancestry. Additionally, many development biologists have accepted that a famous line of evidence supposedly supporting evolution, the notion that "ontogeny recapitulates phylogeny" (the development of an organism replays its evolutionary history), is not supported by developmental data.

Perhaps most importantly, many recently-discovered examples of biological complexity exhibit "irreducible complexity" which could not be built in the step-by-step manner envisioned by Darwin. As our understanding of the cell expands, it is becoming increasingly apparent that Darwinism is incapable of explaining the origin of much biological complexity. This increased knowledge is also forcing scientists to discard what once were thought to be examples of genetic "junk DNA" and vestigial organs which supposedly provide evidence of an undesigned naturalistic evolutionary history. Current trends in biology are revealing complexity beyond that which evolution can produce—the cell is a finely tuned micro-city reflecting what we would expect to be produced by intelligent design.

The IDEA Center believes that naturalistic explanations have their place in explaining the origin of some biological complexity. Evolutionary theory does have some explanatory power, and its useful scope is primarily limited to microevolutionary processes. However, for the most part, naturalistic explanations are incapable of accounting for much of life on Earth.

For more information about problems with naturalistic explanations for the origin and diversification of life, please see:

- Problems with the Origins of Life

- Evolution Primer

- Problems with Evolutionary Explanations of the Fossil Record

- Irreducible Complexity

- Evolution and the Problem of Non-Functional Intermediates

- Design vs. Descent: A War of Predictions

## Darwinism, Naturalism, and Materialistic Philosophy

The fact that science supports a theory which fails to explain so much of the data can only be explained by the fact that a philosophy is preventing scientists from considering new ideas to explain the origin and diversification of life. This philosophy is called "materialism" and is it holds that there were no forces involved in the history of life other than matter, energy, and the chemical and physical laws governing their interactions. Naturalistic explanations often assume that there were no intelligent agents which could have influenced life in the past.

We believe that science should follow the evidence wherever it leads, and should not be constrained by any philosophical presuppositions. Natural explanations may indeed be the best way to explain the origin and diversification of life on Earth. But such hypotheses should be tested—and not assumed. If they are tested with a skeptical mindset, then investigating the origins of life becomes an exciting endeavor where we can test between intelligent design theory and other mechanistic theories of life's origins. The IDEA Center hopes to contribute to this debate and encourage others to participate in this investigation.

| "Whether there is an intelligent designer
| is a matter of religious faith rather
| than a scientifically testable question."

# Intelligent Design
# Is Unscientific

## American Academy for the Advancement of Science

*In this viewpoint the American Academy for the Advancement of Science (AAAS) contends that the consensus among scientists is that the theory of evolution is sound and that intelligent design theory is not scientific. According to the organization, the central tenets of the intelligent design theory—which postulates that an intelligent designer created life—cannot be tested, which all theories must be in order to be considered scientific. AAAS argues that teaching intelligent design in school confuses science with religion, thereby undermining the teaching of science. AAAS, an international organization dedicated to advancing science, publishes* Science *magazine.*

As you read, consider the following questions:

1. What does the word *theory* mean in science, according to AAAS?

American Association for the Advancement of Science, "Q & A on Evolution and Intelligent Design" 2005. Reprinted with permission.

2. According AAAS, what research on intelligent design has been published in relevant scientific journals?

3. What does AAAS say are the two hypothetical claims made under intelligent design theory?

# What is evolution?

Evolution is a broad, well-tested description of how Earth's present-day life forms arose from common ancestors reaching back to the simplest one-celled organisms almost four billion years ago. It helps explain both the similarities and the differences in the enormous number of living organisms we see around us.

By studying the sequence of changes in fossils found in successive layers of rock as well as the molecular evidence provided by modern genetics, scientists have been able to trace how ancient organisms—through a process of descent with modification—gave rise to profound changes in populations over time. Many new anatomical forms have appeared, while others have disappeared. In a very real sense, we are distant genetic cousins to all living organisms, from bacteria to whales.

Evolution occurs in populations when heritable changes are passed from one generation to the next. Genetic variation, whether through random mutations or the gene shuffling that oocurs during sexual reproduction, sets the stage for evolutionary change. That change is driven by forces such as natural selection, in which organisms with advantageous traits, such as color variations in insects that cloak some of them from predators, are better enabled to survive and pass their genes on to future generations.

Ultimately, evolution explains both small-scale changes within populations and large-scale changes in which new species diverge from a common ancestor over many generations.

# "Theory" Defined

*Is evolution "just a theory?"*

In detective novels, a "theory" is little more than an educated guess, often based on a few circumstantial facts. In science, the word "theory" means much more. A scientific theory is a well-substantiated explanation of some aspect of the natural world, based on a body of facts that have been repeatedly confirmed through observation and experiment. Such fact-supported theories are not "guesses" but reliable accounts of the real world. The theory of biological evolution is more than "just a theory." It is as factual an explanation of the universe as the atomic theory of matter or the germ theory of disease. Our undestanding of gravity is still a work in progress. But the phenomenon of gravity, like evolution, is an accepted fact.

*Is there "evidence against" contemporary evolutionary theory?*

No. There are still many puzzles in biology about the particular pathways of the evolutionary process and how various species are related to one another. However, these puzzles neither invalidate nor challenge Darwin's basic theory of "descent with modification" nor the theory's present form that incorporates and is supported by the genetic sciences. Contemporary evolutionary theory provides the conceptual framework in which these puzzles can be addressed and points toward ways to solve them.

*Is there a growing body of scientists who doubt that evolution happened?*

No. The consensus among scientists in many fields, and especially those who study the subject is that contemporary evolutionary theory provides a robust, well-tested explanation for the history of life on earth and for the similarity within the diversity of existing organisms. Very few scientists doubt that evolution happened, although there is lively ongoing inquiry about the details of how it happened. Of the few scientists who criticize contemporary evolutionary theory, most do no research in the field, and so their opinions have little significance for scientists who do.

## The Theory of Intelligent Design

*What is intelligent design?*

"Intelligent design" consists of two hypothetical claims about the history of the universe and of life: first, that some structures or processes in nature are "irreducibly complex" and could not have originated through small changes over long periods of time; and second, that some structures or processes in nature are expressions of "complex specified information" that can only be the product of an intelligent agent.

*Is intelligent design a scientific alternative to contemporary evolutionary theory?*

No. Intelligent design proponents may use the language of science, but they do not use its methodology. They have yet to propose meaningful tests for their claims, there are no reports of current research on these hypotheses at relevant scientific society meetings, and there is no body of research on these hypotheses published in relevant scientific journals. So, intelligent design has not been demonstrated to be a scientific theory. While living things are remarkably complex, scientists have shown that careful, systematic study of them can yield tremendous insights about their functions and origins (as it has in the past).

Intelligent design necessarily presupposes that there is an "intelligent designer" outside of nature who, from the beginning or from time to time, inserts design into the world around us. But whether there is an intelligent designer is a matter of religious faith rather than a scientifically testable question. . . .

## Stifling Debate?

*Are scientists trying to stifle discussion of intelligent design?*

We do not want to censor discussion of intelligent design in the proper setting but the school science classroom is not that setting. Nor do we want to portray evolution as some carved-in-stone dogma. Science is an ongoing process, with new evidence accepted and weighed constantly. Intelligent design advocates have yet to contribute in a scientifically rigorous manner to that process.

AAAS [American Academy for the Advancement of Science] has worked hard to guarantee that children get a first-class science education. We've helped set the objectives for what should be taught and learned in science classrooms. We want to prevent an erosion of the quality of science education. In the case of Kansas, that would be unfortunate at a time when the state is trying to attract high-tech industry and it, like other U.S. states, is trying to nurture more homegrown science talent.

*Are science and religion inherently opposed?*

No. Science does not take a position on an intelligent designer, which is a matter of religious faith, and is not testable scientifically. AAAS and other scientific groups do not want to create the impression that religion and science are inherently in conflict. They live together quite comfortably, including in the minds of many scientists.

Science and religion ask different questions about the world. Many individual scientists are deeply religious. They see scientific investigation and religious faith as complementary components of a well-rounded life.

Ed Stein. Reproduced by permission.

*Can science stimulate religious thought?*

Yes. A particular religion's understanding of the world provides the context from which questions of meaning emerge. A development in science may provide a new more reliable explanation of the structure and processes of the world. This may be different from the understanding of the world that is presumed in a particular religion. What may appear to be a conflict between science and religion is actually a contrast between earlier and more recent understandings of the world (e.g., between an earth-centered universe and a sun-centered universe) and can be a constructive stimulus for religious inquiry. In fact, Jewish, Christian, Muslim, Buddhist and Hindu scholars have sought positive ways to relate evolutionary theory with their religious traditions.

*Is the science classroom the appropriate place to discuss the religious interpretations of science?*

No. Religion is a subject of inquiry in historical, philosophical and social studies, not in science. So, discussion about religion is most appropriate in the social studies or humanities curriculum, not in the science curriculum.

## How Powerful Is the Intelligent Design Movement?

*Have scientists understimated the impact of the intelligent design movement?*

Many scientists probably have been caught unawares, in part, because they don't see an inherent conflict between science and religion. They often are more comfortable in the laboratory doing science and communicating it to students, than they are in the public arena. But it is clear they can no longer afford to ignore the political reality of the intelligent design movement and its effort to sway school boards and curriculum committees in many states and communities. The AAAS is determined to remain engaged on this issue and encourages other scientific groups to do so as well, particularly at the grass roots level.

*What are the stakes?*

The risk, if intelligent design is incorporated into school curricula, is to undermine scientific credibility and the ability of young people to distinguish science from non-science. And that is what matters more, in the longer term, than the specific battles over intelligent design versus evolution. In Kansas, advocates of "intelligent design" are attempting to redefine what is and is not science, in direct conflict with the science standards recommended by both the National Academy of Sciences and AAAS in earlier work. They are pushing the board to reject a definition that limits science to natural explanations for what's observed in the world. They want to define it so that science will include supernatural explanations.

I *"God guided our researchers to discover
the stem cell's power to heal."*

# Embryonic Stem Cell Research Fulfills Christians' Duty to Save Lives

### Nancy Pelosi

*House Democratic Leader Nancy Pelosi argues in this viewpoint
that embryonic stem cell research answers the prayers of families
who have ill family members who could be helped by such
research. Many religious leaders endorse the research, she argues,
because churches have a duty to save human lives. The viewpoint
was taken from remarks delivered by Pelosi after the House of
Representatives adopted the Stem Cell Research Enhancement
Act of 2005, which will increase the number of stem cell lines
that can be researched with federal funds.*

As you read, consider the following questions:

1. What, in the author's view, do science and faith have in
   common?

2. What happens to embryos that are in excess of the

Nancy Pelosi, "With Great Potential of Embryonic Stem Cell Research, Science Has
Power to Answer the Prayers of America's Families," *U.S. Newswire*, May 24, 2005.

needs of in vitro fertilization if they are not used for research, according to Pelosi?

3. What power does the author characterize as "almost biblical"?

This is a critical day for us in Congress. I am deeply indebted to Congresswoman Diana DeGette and Congressman Mike Castle for their great leadership in bringing this bipartisan legislation[1] to the floor.

This is significant legislation because every family in America is just one phone call away, one diagnosis, one accident away from needing the benefits of stem cell research. We want all of the research to proceed—the umbilical cord research, adult stem cell research, that's all very important. But we must have the embryonic stem cell research if we are truly going to be able to have science have the potential it has to cure diseases.

## Miraculous Power of Science

I've served for 10 years on the Labor, Health and Human Services Subcommittee that funds the National Institutes of Health. I've studied this issue through the years, and what we are doing here today is recognizing the miraculous power to cure that exists at the National Institutes of Health and at other institutes of excellence in research throughout our country.

We are recognizing the miraculous, almost biblical, power that science has to cure. And we are here today to say that when these embryos are in excess of the needs of in vitro fertilization, rather than be destroyed, they should be used for basic biomedical research.

1. Pelosi refers to the Stem Cell Research Enhancement Act of 2005, which will increase the number of stem cell lines that can be researched with federal funds. The House passed the bill.

When I first came to the Congress, some of the same people who were against embryonic stem cell research were very much against in vitro fertilization. It's hard to imagine that now, but they were against in vitro fertilization and considered it not to be on high moral ground.

The research is going to occur with federal funding or without. It should not occur without high ethical standards that the federal funding can bring to it.

In order for our country to be pre-eminent in science, we must have the most talented, the most excellent scientists. They will not be attracted to a situation that limits scientific inquiry. As we all know, in science as in business, talent attracts capital, capital that builds all the labs that are needed to do research. And those labs in return attract those excellent scientists, which makes us first in the world, preeminent in science.

I'm particularly proud of my state of California. The people of California in a bipartisan way, as we are doing today, voted a commitment of resources to invest in embryonic stem cell research. We in California will become the regenerative capital of America, indeed probably the world.

This should be happening all over the country; it shouldn't depend on the local initiative of the state. It should be coming from the leadership of the federal government with the ethical standards that go with it.

To some, this debate may seem like a struggle between faith and science. While I have the utmost respect for those who oppose this bill on moral grounds, I believe that faith and science have at least one thing in common: both are searches for truth. America has room for both faith and science.

Indeed, with the great potential of embryonic stem cell research, science has the power to answer the prayers of

---

### A Majority of Americans Approve Stem Cell Research

*"Do you approve or disapprove of medical research using embryonic stem cells?"*

|  | Approve % | Disapprove % | Unsure % |
|---|---|---|---|
| ALL | 56 | 30 | 14 |
| Republicans | 46 | 42 | 12 |
| Demoncrats | 60 | 29 | 11 |
| Independents | 60 | 21 | 19 |
| | | | |
| *Trend:* | | | |
| 5/20–23/05 | 58 | 31 | 11 |
| 8/04 | 50 | 31 | 19 |

SOURCE: CBS News poll, July 13–14, 2005.

---

America's families. I believe strongly in the power of prayer, but part of that prayer is for a cure, and science can provide that.

## Respect for Life

Many religious leaders endorse this bill because of their respect for life and because they believe science, within the bounds of ethics and religious beliefs, can save lives and improve its quality. Groups as diverse as the United Church of Christ, the Union for Reform Judaism, the United Methodist Church, the Episcopal Church USA, and the Union of Orthodox Jewish Congregations of America all support this bill.

The Union of Orthodox Jewish Congregations of America, the nation's largest Orthodox Jewish organization, wrote: 'The traditional Jewish perspective emphasizes the potential to save and heal human lives is an integral part of valuing human life.'

The Episcopal Church in its letter in support of this legislation says, 'As stewards of creation, we are called to help mend and renew the world in many ways. The Episcopal Church celebrates medical research and this research expands our knowledge of God's creation and empowers us to bring potential healing to those who suffer from disease and disability.'

## God Guides Scientists

It is our duty to bring hope to the sick and the disabled, not to bind the hands of those who can bring them hope. I believe God guided our researchers to discover the stem cell's power to heal.

This bill will enable science to live up to its potential to answer the prayers of American families. I urge all of my colleagues to support this bill, and I thank all of my colleagues on both sides of the issue for the dignified approach of how we're dealing with this legislation today.

| *"Human beings are not disposable*
| *biological material."*

# Embryonic Stem Cell Research Destroys Human Lives

**William Saunders**

*William Saunders argues in this viewpoint that research using embryonic stem cells is immoral. Catholic dogma, he says, holds that embryos are human beings from the moment of conception. Because embryos are killed in stem cell research, such research kills human beings. In fact, he says, embryonic stem cell research creates life for the purpose of destroying it. Saunders is a Catholic priest, a professor of theology, and author of* Straight Answers.

As you read, consider the following questions:

1. What other sources of stem cells other than embryos does the author identify that could, in his view, be used for research?

2. How does the author explain the favorable reaction of the public to the pleas of Christopher Reeve and Michael J. Fox for embryonic stem cell research?

William Saunders, "Catholics and Stem-Cell Research," *Arlington Catholic Herald*, October 14, 2004. Reproduced by permission.

3. What other medical procedures does the author cite as also immoral?

The issue concerning stem-cell research certainly has entered the spotlight in the media and has become a very highly politicized issue. The problem is not with the research itself, but from whom one obtains the stem cells. Stem cells are like "master cells" that turn into other types of cells, like nerve, stomach, or brain cells. If one obtains adult stem cells from sources like fat and umbilical cord blood, such research is morally permissible. . . .

On the other hand, stem-cell research may also use embryonic stem cells. These stem cells are obtained by producing an embryo in vitro (i.e. in the laboratory) by fertilizing an ovum, allowing it to develop for a few days in a petri dish, and then extracting the cells, thereby killing the embryo. Such research using embryonic stem cells is immoral.

## Life Begins At Conception

The Catholic Church has consistently asserted that a human being must be respected as a person from the first moment of conception, the very first instance of existence. Each person is made in the image and likeness of God, and thereby has an inherent dignity beyond the rest of creation. The [Vatican's] *Declaration on Procured Abortion* stated:

> From the time that the ovum is fertilized, a new life is begun which is neither that of the father nor of the mother; it is rather the life of a new human being with his own growth. It would never be made human if it were not human already. To this perpetual evidence . . . modern genetic science brings valuable confirmation. It has demonstrated that, from the first instant, the program is fixed as to what this living being will be: a man, this individual man with his characteristic aspects already well determined. Right from fertilization is begun the adventure of human life, and each of its great capacities requires time . . . to find its place and to be in a position to act.

## Grisly Fate for Human Beings

Why not make good use of the extra embryos? Problem is, abortion, in vitro fertilization and embryonic stem cell research are horns springing from the head of the same moral dilemma, because they all involve playing God.

Long story short: In vitro fertilization involves creating multiple embryos in a laboratory and implanting some in a woman's uterus. The rest are either destroyed, stored in freezers or used in experiments—which is a grisly fate for human beings made in God's image.

*Lorraine v. Murray,* Atlanta Journal and Constitution,
*November 6, 2004.*

Moreover, we believe that Almighty God creates and infuses an immortal soul, which truly gives each of us that identity of one made in His image and likeness. Never should any person forget that he or she started life as that one unique cell at the moment of conception.

## Creating Life to Destroy It

Therefore, with embryonic stem-cell research, the subject matter is a person who is purposely created to be destroyed. In 1961, Blessed Pope John XXIII taught, "The transmission of human life is entrusted by nature to a personal and conscious act and as such is subject to the all-holy laws of God: immutable and inviolable laws which must be recognized and observed. Such moral laws include the following: First, a child has a right to be respected as a person from the moment of conception until natural death. Second, a child has the right to be the fruit of the conjugal love of his parents, who are united in marriage. Third, a child has a right to be born.

Given these moral laws, the production of human beings for the sake of experimentation, research, or the harvesting of organs is morally wrong. Human beings are not disposable biological material."

Nevertheless, a great push currently exists for embryonic stem-cell research. This push comes from celebrities with disabilities. Actors Christopher Reeve and Michael J. Fox made many public appearances, even before Congress, promoting embryonic stem-cell research. In their consciences, they must not have been aware that they desire the death of someone else to save their own lives. Yet, their pleas, coupled with their conditions, and especially since Christopher Reeve's death, have pulled at the heartstrings of many people who make moral decisions based on feelings rather than on rational thinking. . . .

## Moral Laws Have Been Abandoned

While we may have the technology "to do" something, we do not necessarily have the moral mandate "to do" something. Just because we can do it, does not mean it ought to be done. Researchers cannot simply think and act as though they are free to do anything without being subject to moral parameters. We find ourselves slipping further down the slope of morality: First came the legislation and proliferation of contraception, then abortion, then *in vitro* fertilization, the cloning of animals and now embryonic stem-cell research. Of course we should not forget the proliferation of doctor-assisted suicide. The moral laws have been abandoned.

Pope John Paul II in his great encyclical *The Gospel of Life (Evangelium Vitae)* taught: "The first and fundamental step towards this cultural transformation consists in forming consciences with regard to the incomparable and inviolable worth of every human life. It is of the greatest importance to re-establish the essential connection between life and freedom. These are inseparable goods: where one is violated, the other also ends up being violated. There is no true freedom where life is not welcomed and loved. . . . No less critical in the formation of conscience is the recovery of the necessary link between freedom and truth. . . . When freedom is detached from objective truth, it becomes impossible to establish personal rights on a first rational basis; and the ground is laid for society to be at the mercy of the unrestrained will of individuals or the oppressive totalitarianism of public authority." The time has come for true Catholics and all Christians to promote genuine freedom and truth in the defense of all human life.

I *"Spirituality is one of our basic human inheritances. It is, in fact, an instinct."*

# Spirituality Is Genetically Determined

*Dean Hamer*

*In this viewpoint, excerpted from his book* The God Gene: How Faith Is Hardwired into Our Genes, *Dean Hamer argues that spirituality is an inheritable instinct. Hamer contends that a specific "God gene" controls brain chemicals that encourage belief in transcendence. He argues that this gene also promotes optimism, which encourages the will to live and reproduce, a competitive evolutionary advantage. Hamer is a geneticist at the National Cancer Institute and author of numerous articles for science journals.*

As you read, consider the following questions:

1. What does the author say is the difference between spiritual instinct and spiritual behavior?

2. How do the brain chemicals called monoamines, in the author's view, influence spirituality?

3. How, according to Hamer, does optimism affect physical life in a positive way?

Why is spirituality such a powerful and universal force? Why do so many people believe in things they cannot see, smell, taste, hear, or touch? Why do people from all walks of life, around the globe, regardless of their religious backgrounds or the particular god they worship, value spirituality as much as, or more than, pleasure, power, or wealth?

I argue that the answer is, at least in part, hardwired into our genes. Spirituality is one of our basic human inheritances. It is, in fact, an instinct.

At first, "instinct" may seem to be a peculiar word to pair with spirituality. We usually think of instincts as automatic, unconscious reactions or behaviors that are performed without thought or training. Birds know to fly south for the winter by instinct. Blinking your eyes when someone takes a swing at you is an instinct. A newborn baby learns to suckle at her mother's breast by instinct, not because she has been taught. It is instinctual to become aroused when presented with a sexual stimulus. By contrast, spiritual *behaviors* such as meditating in the lotus position or taking communion are neither automatic nor unconscious. They are highly deliberate and culturally learned activities.

I do not contend that spirituality is a simple instinct like blinking or nursing. But I do argue that it is a complex amalgamation in which certain genetically hardwired, biological patterns of response and states of consciousness are interwoven with social, cultural, and historical threads. It is this interdigitation of biology and experience that makes spirituality such a durable part of the fabric of life—a rich tapestry in which nature is the warp and nurture is the woof.

## Nature and Nurture

The idea of complex characteristics that are influenced by both genes and environment is not unique to spirituality. There are many well-known examples of the interplay between nature and nurture, even among animals. Consider the song of the white-crowned sparrow. The male sparrow's song, which he begins to sing at about seven or eight months of age, consists of a long, low whistle followed by a series of trills. That the song is at least partly innate can be seen by its species specificity: All male white-crowned sparrows sing basically the same song, even when they are separated from their parents after two weeks and raised in complete isolation from any other birds. Moreover, there is a dedicated brain circuit for song, consisting of six interconnected brain regions that control the vibrations of the vocal membranes in the throat. (Three of the regions are sensitive to sex hormones, which explains why only males produce the characteristic mating song.) The reason a sparrow sings the song of a sparrow, and not of a robin or a lark, is that it has the genes and brain of a sparrow, not that it was raised by sparrows.

But experiments show that the song is also partly learned. Sparrows from different areas sing slightly different varieties of the song, or "dialects," that differ in the exact number and placement of the trill notes. When sparrows are left with their parents for the first three months of life, then raised in isolation or with foster parents from another region, they still sing the parental dialect when they begin to vocalize a few months later. By contrast, when the young birds are taken from the nest after only a few weeks, then raised hearing tape recordings of a different dialect, they sing the foreign song.

An even more profound effect of the environment has been shown in studies in which the chicks have been deafened at an early age. These poor animals never produce anything more than a few unconnected notes, no matter how hard they try. They need to hear themselves to sing properly.

Such experiments show that while the basic species-specific skeleton of the song is hardwired in the genes, it requires the environmental due of being able to hear its own voice to be triggered. And while the precise details of the song are culturally transmitted during a critical period early in life, they require the right biological machinery and genetic code to be actualized. It's part of the remarkable yin and yang of nature and nurture, especially in a species that most people would never even associate with having a culture.

## A Predisposition for Spiritual Belief

In *The God Gene*, I propose that spirituality has a biological mechanism akin to birdsong, albeit a far more complex and nuanced one: that we have a genetic predisposition for spiritual belief that is expressed in response to, and shaped by, personal experience and the cultural environment. These genes, I argue, act by influencing the brain's capability for various types and forms of consciousness, which become the basis for spiritual experiences.

The term "God gene" is, in fact, a gross oversimplification of the theory. There are probably many different genes involved, rather than just one. And environmental influences are just as important as genetics. Finally, spirituality, in its broader meaning, is about much more than belief in a particular God. Some of the most spiritual people I've interviewed. . .don't believe in a deity at all. Nevertheless, I felt it was a useful abbreviation of the overall concept.

## Measuring Spirituality

Proving there is a genetic component to spirituality is no simple task, and probably no single line of evidence or observation will be completely convincing. It's not like hair or eye color, which are passed from one generation to the next in an obvious way. Therefore, I use several different lines of reasoning and types of data in the book to show the instinctual

## Buddhism and the God Gene

Buddhists, says Robert Thurman, professor of Buddhist studies at Columbia University, have long entertained the idea that we inherit a spirituality gene from the person we were in a previous life. Smaller than an ordinary gene, it combines with two larger physical genes we inherit from our parents, and together they shape our physical and spiritual profile. Says Thurman: "The spiritual gene helps establish a general trust in the universe, a sense of openness and generosity."

*Jeffrey Kluger,* Time International, *October 25, 2004.*

side of spirituality. Some of them are based in traditional approaches to religion such as psychology and anthropology. The main emphasis, however, is on powerful new research methods that have been developed in molecular genetics and neurobiology. The proof, in other words, depends on the whole pudding—the entire array of evidence—not just one ingredient. Let me summarize the five essential arguments I intend to present:

*Measurement.* The first task for any scientist attempting to link genetics to spirituality is to show that spirituality can be defined and quantitated. This is essential for any scientific analysis, regardless of the topic. Scientists measure things. If we can't measure it, we can't test a hypothesis about it, and if we can't test a hypothesis, it can't be proved.

Measuring spirituality is particularly difficult because it encompasses so many different types of feelings, beliefs, and experiences. Fortunately, a number of psychologists have tackled the problem using sophisticated statistical methods of psychological measurement. In the book, I use a scale called "self-transcendence" developed by Robert Cloninger, an innovative thinker who studies the biological and social origins of personality.

Self-transcendence provides a numerical measure of people's capacity to reach out beyond themselves—to see everything in the world as part of one great totality. If I were to describe it in a single word, it might be "at-one-ness."

Although self-transcendence might seem a bit "flaky" to some readers, it successfully passes the tests for a solid psychological trait. It basically is a yardstick for what is often referred to in the West as *faith*, or in the East as the search for *enlightenment*.

One of my biggest challenges in *The God Gene* is to attempt to separate spirituality from religion. This is difficult because religion is founded on spiritual beliefs. Conversely, spiritual beliefs usually are expressed using the language and rituals of religion. Nevertheless, the self-transcendence scale tries to separate one's spirituality from one's particular religious beliefs by eschewing questions about belief in a particular God, frequency of prayer, or other orthodox religious doctrines or practices. Even individuals who dislike all forms of organized religion may have a strong spiritual capacity and score high on the self-transcendence scale. . . .

*Heritability.* The next task for the scientist exploring the link between genetics and spirituality is to determine whether spirituality is inherited, and if so, to what extent. This can be tackled by using twin studies—comparing identical twins, who have the exact same genes, to fraternal twins, who are only as genetically similar as ordinary siblings. One can determine a factor's *heritability* by comparing resemblances and differences between different types of twins, and between twins and unrelated people.

Scientists have used twin studies to show that spirituality, as measured by the self-transcendence scale, is significantly heritable. The extent of genetic influence is similar to that for many personality traits, and even greater than it is for some physical characteristics. In other words, there is a strong genetic link.

Twin studies also can be used to study the role of the environment on a trait or behavior. Not surprisingly, upbringing plays an important role in spirituality. But remarkably, what counts most is not the specific shared cultural environment, such as Sunday school, sermons, or parenting. What is important are the unique life events each person experiences on their own.

## Genes and Chemistry

*Identifying a Specific Gene.* While twin studies suggest that spirituality is partially inherited, they say nothing about which genes are involved or how they work. That's the job of molecular biology. One major new finding revealed in *The God Gene* is our discovery of a specific individual gene associated with the self-transcendence scale of spirituality. This "God gene" codes for a monoamine transporter—a protein that controls the amount of crucial brain signaling chemicals. Interestingly, these same brain chemicals can be triggered by certain drugs that can bring about mystical-like experiences.

The specific gene I have identified is by no means the entire story behind spirituality. It plays only a small, if key, role; many other genes and environmental factors also are involved. Nevertheless, the gene is important because it points out the mechanism by which spirituality is manifested in the brain.

*Brain Mechanism.* The monoamines I identify—the brain chemicals controlled by the God gene—have many different functions in the brain. They appear to influence spirituality by altering consciousness, which can be broadly defined as our

145

sense of reality—our awareness of ourselves and the universe around us, including our thoughts, memories, and perceptions.

The intimate relationship between spirituality and consciousness becomes most conspicuous through mystical experiences, such as Saul's conversion on the road to Damascus, which are invariably accompanied by major alterations in perceptions. But the relationship between spirituality and consciousness also is evident in more subtle forms, such as self-transcendence, in which consciousness is altered by a blurring of the normal distinction between self and other.

Monoamines such as serotonin and dopamine are important players in consciousness. According to a theory developed by Gerald Edelman, the key role of monoamines with regard to consciousness is to link objects and experiences with emotions and values. Evidence supporting the importance of monoamines in affecting consciousness may be seen with the help of sophisticated brain-scanning techniques and by analyzing the actions of various types of drugs that block or enhance these brain chemicals, as well as in studies of individuals with brain lesions such as temporal lobe epilepsy.

*Selective Advantage.* Darwin's theory of evolution and competitive advantage applies as much to complex human behavioral characteristics such as spirituality as it does to beak shape in birds or hunting ability in lions. What are the selective advantages of having God genes? Are they simply a side effect of the evolution of the mind, or do they offer us a more direct evolutionary advantage?

I argue that one of the important roles that God genes play in natural selection is to provide human beings with an innate sense of optimism. At the psychological level, optimism is the will to keep on living and procreating, despite the fact that death is ultimately inevitable. At the physical level, studies show that optimism seems to promote better health and quicker recovery from disease, advantages that would help us live long enough to have and raise children and pass on our genetic heritage.

*"It is reasonable to ask, as ['God gene'
advocate Dean] Hamer does, whether
certain genes play a significant role in
faith. But he is a long way from providing an answer."*

# Evidence That Spirituality
# Is Genetically Determined
# Is Weak

*Carl Zimmer*

*In this critique of Dean Hamer's theory that a "God gene" is
responsible for spirituality, Carl Zimmer argues that the evidence
presented in support of the theory is both slight and untested. In
fact, Zimmer claims, Hamer's theory is mostly untested specula-
tion. Zimmer argues that claims of a genetic basis for spirituality
would need to be tested for a decade before such a theory could
become plausible. Zimmer is the author of* At the Water's Edge
*and a columnist for* Natural History.

As you read, consider the following questions:

1. What is the name of the gene identified by Hamer as

the "God gene"?

2. According to the author, what evidence, in addition to Hamer's book, supports the theory of a "God gene"?

3. The author describes a study linking genes with male homosexuality that could not be replicated by other scientists. Who authored that study?

By page 77 of *The God Gene*, Dean H. Hamer has already disowned the title of his own book. He recalls describing to a colleague his discovery of a link between spirituality and a specific gene he calls "the God gene." His colleague raised her eyebrows. "Do you mean there's just one?" she asked.

"I deserved her skepticism," Hamer writes. "What I meant to say, of course, was 'a' God gene, not 'the' God gene."

Of course. Why, the reader wonders, didn't Hamer call his book *A God Gene*? That might not have been as catchy, but at least it wouldn't have left him contradicting himself.

Whatever you want to call it, this is a frustrating book. The role that genes play in religion is a fascinating question that's ripe for the asking. Psychologists, neurologists and even evolutionary biologists have offered insights about how spiritual behaviors and beliefs emerge from the brain. It is reasonable to ask, as Hamer does, whether certain genes play a significant role in faith. But he is a long way from providing an answer.

## The Path Hamer Travelled

Hamer, a geneticist at the National Cancer Institute, wound up on his quest for the God gene by a roundabout route. Initially he and his colleagues set out to find genes that may make people prone to cigarette addiction. They studied hundreds of pairs of siblings, comparing how strongly their shared heredity influenced different aspects of their personality. In addition to having their subjects fill out psychological

## Reductionist Thinking

Our most profound feelings of spirituality, according to a literal reading of [Dean] Hamer's work, may be due to little more than an occasional shot of intoxicating brain chemicals governed by our DNA. "I'm a believer that every thought we think and every feeling we feel is the result of activity in the brain," Hamer says. "I think we follow the basic law of nature, which is that we're a bunch of chemical reactions running around in a bag."

Even for the casually religious, such seeming reductionism can rankle. The very meaning of faith, after all, is to hold fast to something without all the tidy cause and effect that science finds so necessary. Try parsing things the way geneticists do, and you risk parsing them into dust. "God is not something that can be demonstrated logically or rigorously," says Neil Gillman, a professor of Jewish philosophy at the Jewish Theological Seminary in New York City. "[The idea of a God gene] goes against all my personal theological convictions." John Polkinghorne, a physicist who is also Canon Theologian at England's Liverpool Cathedral, agrees: "You can't cut [faith] down to the lowest common denominator of genetic survival. It shows the poverty of reductionist thinking."

*Jeffrey Kluger,* Time International, *October 25, 2004.*

questionnaires, the researchers also took samples of DNA from some of them. Hamer then realized that this database might let him investigate the genetics of spirituality.

He embarked on this new search by looking at the results of certain survey questions that measured a personality trait known as self-transcendence, originally identified by Washington University psychiatrist Robert Cloninger. Cloninger found that spiritual people tend to share a set of characteristics, such as feeling connected to the world and a willingness to accept things that cannot be objectively demonstrated. Analyzing the cigarette study, Hamer confirmed what earlier studies had found: heredity is partly responsible for whether a person is self-transcendent or not. He then looked at the DNA samples of some of his subjects, hoping to find variants of genes that tended to turn up in self-transcendent people.

His search led him to a gene known as VMAT2. Two different versions of this gene exist, differing only at a single position. People with one version of the gene tend to score a little higher on self-transcendence tests. Although the influence is small, it is, Hamer claims, consistent. About half the people in the study had at least one copy of the self-transcendence-boosting version of VMAT2, which Hamer dubs the God gene.

## Testing the Theory

Is the God gene real? The only evidence we have to go on at the moment is what Hamer presents in his book. He and his colleagues are still preparing to submit their results to a scientific journal. It would be nice to know whether these results can withstand the rigors of peer review. It would be nicer still to know whether any other scientists can replicate them. The field of behavioral genetics is littered with failed links between particular genes and personality traits. These alleged associations at first seemed very strong. But as other researchers tried to replicate them, they faded away into statistical noise. In 1993, for example, a scientist reported a genetic link to male homosexuality in a region of the X chromosome. The report brought a huge media fanfare, but other scientists who tried to replicate the study failed. The scientist's name was Dean Hamer.

To be fair, it should be pointed out that Hamer offers a lot of details about his study in *The God Gene*, along with many caveats about how hard it is to establish an association between genes and behavior. But given the fate of Hamer's so-called gay gene, it is strange to see him so impatient to trumpet the discovery of his God gene. He is even eager to present an intricate hypothesis about how the God gene produces self-transcendence. The gene, it is well known, makes membrane-covered containers that neurons use to deliver neurotransmitters to one another. Hamer proposes that the God gene changes the level of these neurotransmitters so as to alter a person's mood, consciousness and, ultimately, self-transcendence. He goes so far as to say that the God gene is, along with other faith-boosting genes, a product of natural selection. Self-transcendence makes people more optimistic, which makes them healthier and likely to have more kids.

## Little Support for the Theory

These speculations take up the bulk of *The God Gene*, but in support Hamer only offers up bits and pieces of research done by other scientists, along with little sketches of spiritual people he has met. It appears that he has not bothered to think of a way to test these ideas himself. He did not, for example, try to rule out the possibility that natural selection has not favored self-transcendence, but some other function of VMAT2. (Among other things, the gene protects the brain from neurotoxins.) Nor does Hamer rule out the possibility that the God gene offers no evolutionary benefit at all. Sometimes genes that seem to be common thanks to natural selection turn out to have been spread merely by random genetic drift.

Rather than address these important questions, Hamer simply declares that any hypothesis about the evolution of human behavior must be purely speculative. But this is simply not true. If Hamer wanted, he could have measured the strength of natural selection that has acted on VMAT2 in the past. And if he did find signs of selection, he could have estimated how long ago it took place. Other scientists have been measuring natural selection this way for several years now and publishing their results in major journals.

*The God Gene* might have been a fascinating, enlightening book if Hamer had written it 10 years from now—after his link between VMAT2 and self-transcendence had been confirmed by others and after he had seriously tested its importance to our species. Instead the book we have today would be better titled: *A Gene That Accounts for Less Than One Percent of the Variance Found in Scores on Psychological Questionnaires Designed to Measure a Factor Called Self-Transcendence, Which Can Signify Everything from Belonging to the Green Party to Believing in ESP, According to One Unpublished, Unreplicated Study.*

# Periodical Bibliography

The following articles have been selected to supplement the diverse views in this chapter:

John S. Bowker "Will Religion Become Irrelevant? If Religion Does Not Accommodate Scientific Advances, It Will Be Pushed to the Margins," *Science & Theology News*, May 20, 2005.

Robert Roy Britt "Scientists' Belief in God Varies Starkly by Discipline," *LiveScience.com*, August 11, 2005. www.livescience.com.

Alan Cutler "The War That Wasn't: Science and Religion Have Often Stood Together," *Washington Post*, January 8, 2006.

Christl Dabu "Stem-Cell Science Stirs Debate in Muslim World, Too," *Christian Science Monitor*, June 22, 2005.

Muzaffar Iqbal "The International Religion-Science Discourse: Pitfalls, Obstacles, and Opportunities," *Islam and Science*, December 22, 2005.

Marilyn Karfeld "Intelligent Design: Religion or Science?" *Cleveland Jewish News*, January 13, 2006.

Eric Mink "Faith and Science Aren't Mutually Exclusive, Intelligent-Design Hucksters Are Twisting the Discussion to Sneak Religion into Public Schools," *St. Louis Post-Dispatch*, August 31, 2005.

Corie Pikul "Church OK's Condoms in AIDS Fight," Inter Press Service English News Wire, March 7, 2005.

CHAPTER 4

# Is Religious Fundamentalism a Serious Problem?

# Chapter Preface

The term "fundamentalism" originated in a series of pamphlets published by evangelical churchmen between 1910 and 1915 called *The Fundamentals: A Testimony to the Truth.* Fundamentalism was a conservative response to liberalizing trends in many Christian churches and to Charles Darwin's theory of evolution, whose tenets seemed to contradict biblical stories about how life on earth came about. Today, the term often is used in the West to refer to religious individuals or groups who believe in a literal and traditional interpretation of sacred texts. Scholar Karen Armstrong observes that fundamentalism erupted in every major religion in the world during the twentieth century and "represents a kind of revolt or rebellion against the secular hegemony of the modern world. Fundamentalists typically want to see God, or religion, reflected more centrally in public life."

As fundamentalism has increased, scholars have worked to refine a definition for the term that applies across religions. Ken Decks, academic dean of Christ for Nations College, says that fundamentalists can be defined by four features: (1) belief in a single set of religious teachings that contains the essential and inerrant truth about humanity and God; (2) a belief that this truth is opposed by forces of evil that must be fought; (3) a belief that this truth must be followed today according to the unchangeable practices of the past; and (4) conviction that those who believe in this truth have a special relationship with God. Whether these features make fundamentalists agents of good or evil is the subject of intense debate.

Many people think of fundamentalism in negative terms. These analysts claim that fundamentalists often take extreme measures to impose their views on others. Author and theologian Martin E. Marty observes that deadly violence often occurs when brands of fundamentalism clash, as in the case of religiously motivated Jewish settlers and Islamic militants fighting for the same territory on the West Bank and Gaza [in Israel]. In Africa, a bitter contest for souls between Christianity and Islam has led to the torture, murder, and, reportedly, the crucifixion of Christians by Islamic extremists. In Pakistan, blasphemy laws putatively based in Islamic law are used to justify the persecution of Christians and other religious minorities.

Perhaps also notable is the fact that the September 11, 2001, terrorist attacks against the United States were perpetrated by Islamic extremists bent on destroying America, which the terrorists consider a decadent nation.

Despite the negative associations, many commentators note that fundamentalism is not inherently bad. Richard Antoun, author of *Understanding Fundamentalism: Christian, Islamic and Jewish Movements*, observes that

> fundamentalism is no more irrational than any other ideology; and given their assumptions, fundamentalists are just as rational as anybody else. They demonstrate so by their acceptance of many aspects of the modern world such as bureaucratic organization, business norms, and technology. They are people who function in the modern world, and are usually very successful.

Moreover, these analysts note, fundamentalist views offer a stabilizing sense of morality to people of faith during a time of perplexing change, when ethics seem to be in decline. For example, fundamentalists work to stabilize the institution of marriage, which many believe is the cornerstone of society.

Fundamentalism has become the subject of heated debate as increasingly more people identify with fundamentalist tenets. In the following chapter authors explore the nature of religious fundamentalism, making cases for and against the claim that fundamentalism poses a serious threat to world peace and social order.

> "One who carries out a martyrdom
> operation [suicide bombing] has a
> clear goal, and that is to please Allah."

# The Koran Permits Martyrdom Bombing

*Yousef al-Qaradhawi*

*In this viewpoint Yousef al-Qaradhawi argues that "suicide bombings" should not be considered terrorism or suicide but instead martyrdom operations that are necessary to repel invaders of Islamic lands. He argues that the unintended death of children or innocent Muslims in such bombings are an unfortunate but permitted necessity of war. Yousef al-Qaradhawi is an influential Sunni Muslim cleric and head of the European Council for Fatwa and Research (ECFR). This viewpoint is based upon a report he gave to ECFR.*

As you read, consider the following questions:

1. What unique trait does the author say makes Israeli society different from other societies?

2. Why are the "blood and property" of those who do not

Yousef al-Qaradhawi, "Al-Qaradhawi Speaks in Favor of Suicide Operations at an Islamic Conference in Sweden," *Middle East Media Research Institute*, July 24, 2003. Reproduced by permission.

believe in Islam not worthy of protection, according to the author?

3. How, in the author's view, is suicide different from the goals of martyrdom?

The martyrdom operations carried out by the Palestinian factions to resist the Zionist occupation [of Palestinian lands] are not in any way included in the framework of prohibited terrorism, even if the victims include some civilians.

This is for several reasons.

First of all, due to the colonialist, occupational, racist, and [plundering] nature of Israeli society, it is, in fact, a military society. Anyone past childhood, man or woman, is drafted into the Israeli army.[1] Every Israeli is a solider in the army, either in practical terms or because he is a reservist soldier who can be summoned at any time for war. This fact needs no proof. Those they call 'civilians' are in effect 'soldiers' in the army of the sons of Zion.

## Israel Is an Invader

Second, Israeli society has a unique trait that makes it different from the other human societies, and that is that as far as the people of Palestine are concerned, it is a 'society of invaders' who came from outside the region—from Russia or America, from Europe or from the lands of the Orient—to occupy Palestine and settle in it. . . .

Those who are invaded have the right to fight the invaders with all means at their disposal in order to remove [the invaders] from their homes and send them back to the homes from whence they came. . . . This is a *Jihad* [holy war] of necessity, as the clerics call it, and not *Jihad* of choice. . . . Even if an in-

---

1. The author is incorrect. Few women serve as reservists in the Israeli army.

nocent child is killed as a result of this *Jihad*—it was not intended, but rather due to the necessities of the war. . . . Even with the passage of time, these [Israeli] so-called 'civilians' do not stop being invaders, evil, tyrants, and oppressors. . . .

Third . . . it has been determined by Islamic law that the blood and property of people of *Dar Al-Harb* [the Domain of Disbelief where the battle for the domination of Islam should be waged] is not protected. Because they fight against and are hostile towards the Muslims, they annulled the protection of their blood and their property.

Fourth, the Muslim clerics, or most of them, have agreed that it is permissible to kill Muslims if the army that attacks the Muslims hides behind them, that is, uses them as barricades or human shields, and sets them at the front so that the fire, arrows, or spears of the Muslims will harm them first. The clerics have permitted the defenders to kill these innocent Muslims, who were forced to stand at the head of the army of their enemies . . . otherwise the invading army will enter and annihilate their offspring and their harvests. There was no choice but to sacrifice some [of the Muslims] in order to defend the entire [Muslim] community. . . . Therefore, if it is permitted to kill innocent Muslims who are under coercion in order to protect the greater Muslim community, it is all the more so permissible to kill non-Muslims in order to liberate the land of the Muslims from its occupiers and oppressors.

Fifth, in modern war, all of society, with all its classes and ethnic groups, is mobilized to participate in the war, to aid its continuation, and to provide it with the material and human fuel required for it to assure the victory of the state fighting its enemies. Every citizen in society must take upon himself a role in the effort to provide for the battle. The entire domestic front, including professionals, laborers, and industrialists, stands behind the fighting army, even if it does not bear arms. Therefore the experts say that the Zionist entity, in truth, is one army.

## Extreme Necessity

Sixth, there are two types of *Fatwas: Fatwas*[2] concerning a situation of calm and choice, and *Fatwas* concerning a situation of distress and necessity. It is permissible for a Muslim, when in a situation of extreme necessity, to do what is prohibited to him [in circumstances allowing] choice. . . . Thus, one of the clerics has espoused the rule: 'Necessities permit prohibitions.' Our brothers in Palestine are, without a doubt, in a situation of extreme necessity to carry out martyrdom operations in order to unsettle their enemies and the plunderers of their land and to sow horror in their hearts so that they will leave, and return to the places from whence they came. . . .

What weapon can harm their enemy, can prevent him from sleeping, and can strip him of a sense of security and stability, except for these human bombs—a young man or woman who blows himself or herself up amongst their enemy. This is a weapon the likes of which the enemy cannot obtain, even if the U.S. provides it with billions [of dollars] and the most powerful weapons, because it is a unique weapon that Allah has placed only in the hands of the men of belief. It is a type of divine justice on the face of the earth . . . it is the weapon of the wretched weak in the face of the powerful tyrant. . . .

## Martyrdom, Not Suicide

Those who oppose martyrdom operations and claim that they are suicide are making a great mistake. The goals of the one who carries out a martyrdom operation and of the one who commits suicide are completely different. Anyone who analyzes the soul of [these two] will discover the huge difference between them. The [person who commits] suicide kills himself for himself, because he failed in business, love, an examina-

---

2. Fatwa is a legal pronouncement issued by a qualified Islamic law specialist.

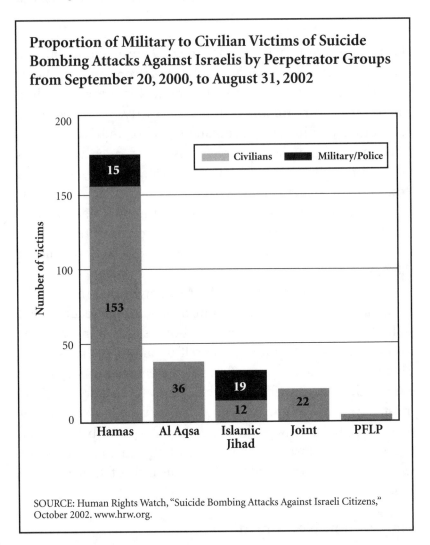

**Proportion of Military to Civilian Victims of Suicide Bombing Attacks Against Israelis by Perpetrator Groups from September 20, 2000, to August 31, 2002**

SOURCE: Human Rights Watch, "Suicide Bombing Attacks Against Israeli Citizens," October 2002. www.hrw.org.

tion, or the like. He was too weak to cope with the situation and chose to flee life for death.

In contrast, the one who carries out a martyrdom operation does not think of himself. He sacrifices himself for the sake of a higher goal, for which all sacrifices become meaningless. He sells himself to Allah in order to buy Paradise in exchange. Allah said: "Allah has bought from the believers their souls and their properties for they shall inherit Paradise."

While the [person who commits] suicide dies in escape and retreat, the one who carries out a martyrdom operation dies in advance and attack. Unlike the [person who commits] suicide, who has no goal except escape from confrontation, the one who carries out a martyrdom operation has a clear goal, and that is to please Allah. . . .

Suicide bombings *"are not just crimes against humanity and against civiliza-tion; they are also acts—from a Muslim point of view—of blasphemy."*

# The Koran Forbids Suicide Bombing

### Bernard Lewis

*Bernard Lewis, in the following viewpoint, argues that suicide bombing and the killing of innocents are historically recent developments without precedent or justification in Islamic law. Citing passages from writings about the Prophet Mohammad, the author claims that Islam views suicide as a major sin merit-ing eternal damnation. Lewis is a professor of Near Eastern studies at Princeton University and author of many books about the Middle East.*

As you read, consider the following questions:

1. How does the author say nationalist terrorists of the 1960s and 1970s differ from the ones who carried out the September 11, 2001, terrorist attacks?

Bernard Lewis, *The Crisis of Islam: Unholy War and Unholy Terror*, New York, NY: The Modern Library, 2002. Copyright © 2002 by Bernard Lewis. Used by permission of Modern Library, a division of Random House, Inc.

2. What groups pioneered Islamic suicide missions, according to the author?

3. In the view of the author, are the September 11 terrorist attacks blasphemous according to the beliefs of Islam?

A new phase in religious mobilization began with the movement known in Western languages as pan-Islamism. Launched in the 1960s and '70s, it probably owed something to the examples of the Germans and the Italians in their successful struggles for national unification in those years. Their Muslim contemporaries and imitators inevitably identified themselves and defined their objectives in religious and communal rather than nationalist or patriotic terms, which at that time were still alien and unfamiliar. But with the spread of European influence and education, these ideas took root and for a while dominated both discourse and struggle in the Muslim lands. Yet the religious identity and loyalty were still deeply felt, and they found expression in several religious movements, notably the Muslim Brothers. With the resounding failure of secular ideologies, they acquired a new importance, and these movements took over the fight—and many of the fighters—from the failed nationalists.

For the fundamentalists as for the nationalists, the various territorial issues are important but in a different, more intractable form. For example, for the fundamentalists in general, no peace or compromise with Israel is possible, and any concession is only a step toward the true final solution— the dissolution of the State of Israel, the return of the land of Palestine to its true owners, the Muslim Palestinians, and the departure of the intruders. Yet this would by no means satisfy the fundamentalists' demands, which extend to all the other disputed territories—and even their acquisition would only be a step toward the longer, final struggle.

Much of the old tactic was retained, but in a significantly more vigorous form. Both in defeat and in victory, the religious terrorists adopted and improved on the methods pioneered by the nationalists of the twentieth century, in particular the lack of concern at the slaughter of innocent bystanders. This unconcern reached new proportions in the terror campaign launched by Usama bin Ladin in the early 1990s. The first major example was the bombing of two American embassies in East Africa in 1998. In order to kill twelve American diplomats, the terrorists were willing to slaughter more than two hundred Africans, many of them Muslims, who happened to be in the vicinity. In its issue immediately after these attacks, an Arabic-language fundamentalist magazine called *Al-Sirt al-Mustaqm*, published in Pittsburgh, Pennsylvania, expressed its mourning for the "martyrs" who gave their lives in these operations and listed their names, as supplied by the office of Al-Qa'ida in Peshawar, Pakistan. The writer added an expression of hope "that God would. . .reunite us with them in paradise." The same disregard for human life, on a vastly greater scale, underlay the actions in New York and Washington on September 11, 2001.

## Suicide Terrorists

A significant figure in these operations was the suicide terrorist. In one sense, this was a new development. The nationalist terrorists of the 1960s and '70s generally took care not to die along with their victims but arranged to carry out their attacks from a safe distance. If they had the misfortune to be captured, their organizations usually tried, sometimes successfully, to obtain their release by seizing hostages and threatening to harm or kill them. Earlier religiously inspired murderers, notably the Assassins, disdained to survive their operations but did not actually kill themselves. The same may be said of the Iranian boy soldiers in the 1980–1988 war against Iraq, who walked through minefields, armed only with a passport to paradise, to clear the way for the regular troops.

## Grave Sin

If killing oneself is viewed with horror, it is even more horrendous to kill civilians as part of the destructive act of suicide bombing. Killing another innocent human being deliberately is murder. The Koran says if one kills another human being unjustly, it is as grave a sin as killing all of humanity.

Even in the case of war, the Prophet Mohammed gave clear instructions to Muslims that noncombatants should not be targeted. He included in this category women, children and people not directly involved in fighting. Today's suicide bombers have conveniently ignored all such instructions.

*Abdullah Saeed*, Australian, *July 16, 2005.*

The new type of suicide mission in the strict sense of the word seems to have been pioneered by religious organizations like Hamas and Hizbullah, who from 1982 onward carried out a number of such missions in Lebanon and in Israel. They continued through the 1980s and '90s, with echoes in other areas, for example in eastern Turkey, in Egypt, in India, and in Sri Lanka. From the information available, it would seem that the candidates chosen for these missions were, with occasional exceptions, male, young, and poor, often from refugee camps. They were offered a double reward—in the afterlife, the minutely described delights of paradise; in this world, bounties and stipends for their families. A remarkable innovation was the use of female suicide bombers—by Kurdish terrorists in Turkey in 1996–1999, and by Palestinians from January 2002.

Unlike the medieval holy warrior or Assassin, who was willing to face certain death at the hands of his enemies or captors, the new suicide terrorist dies by his own hand. This raises an important question of Islamic teaching. Islamic law books are very clear on the subject of suicide. It is a major sin and is punished by eternal damnation in the form of the endless repetition of the act by which the suicide killed himself. The following passages, from the traditions of the Prophet, make the point vividly:

> The Prophet said: Whoever kills himself with a blade will be tormented with that blade in the fires of Hell.

> The Prophet also said: He who strangles himself will strangle himself in Hell, and he who stabs himself will stab himself in Hell. . . . He who throws himself off a mountain and kills himself will throw himself downward into the fires of Hell for ever and ever. He who drinks poison and kills himself will carry his poison in his hand and drink it in Hell for ever and ever. . . . Whoever kills himself in any way will be tormented in that way in Hell. . . . Whoever kills himself in any way in this world will be tormented with it on the day of resurrection.

The early authorities make a clear distinction between facing certain death at the hands of the enemy and dying by one's own hand. A very early tradition of the type known as *hadīth qudsī*, denoting a statement of the Prophet citing God Himself, gives a striking example. The Prophet was present when a man mortally wounded in the holy war killed himself to shorten his pain. Whereupon God said: "My servant preempted me by taking his soul with his own hand; he will therefore not be admitted to paradise." According to another early tradition, the Prophet refused to say prayers over the body of a man who had died by his own hand.

Two features mark the attacks of September 11 and other similar actions: the willingness of the perpetrators to commit suicide and the ruthlessness of those who send them, concerning both their own emissaries and their numerous victims. Can these in any sense be justified in terms of Islam?

The answer must be a clear no.

## No Precedence

The callous destruction of thousands in the World Trade Center, including many who were not American, some of them Muslims from Muslim countries, has no justification in Islamic doctrine or law and no precedent in Islamic history. Indeed, there are few acts of comparable deliberate and indiscriminate wickedness in human history. These are not just crimes against humanity and against civilization; they are also acts—from a Muslim point of view—of blasphemy, when those who perpetrate such crimes claim to be doing so in the name of God, His Prophet, and His scriptures.

The response of many Arabs and Muslims to the attack on the World Trade Center was one of shock and horror at the terrible destruction and carnage, together with shame and anger that this was being done in their name and in the name of their faith. This was the response of many—but not all. There were reports and even pictures of rejoicing in the streets in Arab and other Muslim cities at the news from New York. In part, the reaction was one of envy—a sentiment that was also widespread, in a more muted form, in Europe. Among the poor and the wretched there was a measure of satisfaction—for some indeed of delight—in seeing the rich and self-indulgent Americans being taught a lesson.

> "Right-wing religion . . . not only legitimates intolerance and anti-democratic forms of religious correctness, it also lays the groundwork for a growing authoritarianism."

# Christian Fundamentalism Threatens Democracy in the United States

*Henry A. Giroux*

*In this viewpoint Henry A. Giroux argues that American Christian fundamentalists believe that only they know the truth, and they see those who disagree with them as evil. Giroux argues that Christian fundamentalism has replaced critical thought with anti-intellectual authoritarianism. He also claims that Christian fundamentalists in government promote intolerance and holy wars against non-Christians. Giroux is author of* The Terror of Neoliberalism.

As you read, consider the following questions:

1. According to Giroux, what has one conservative

Henry A. Giroux, "The Passion of the Right: Religious Fundamentalism and the Growing Threat to Democracy," *Dissident Voice*, November 29, 2004. Reproduced by permission of www.dissidentvoice.org.

Christian senator proposed as punishment for doctors performing abortions?

2. As stated by the author, what did Republicans, during the 2004 presidential elections, claim Democrats were going to do in Arkansas and West Virginia?

3. What were evangelical marines doing to prepare for battle in Iraq, according to the author?

With the re-election of George W. Bush, religious fundamentalism seems to be in overdrive in its effort to define politics through a reductive and somewhat fanatical moralism. This kind of religious zealotry has a long tradition in American history extending from the arrival of Puritanism in the seventeenth century to the current spread of Pentecostalism. This often ignored history, imbued with theocratic certainty and absolute moralism, has been quite powerful in providing religious justification to the likes of the Ku Klux Klan, the parlance of the Robber Barons, the patriarchal imbued discourse of "family values," and the recent spectacle of Mel Gibson's cinematic display of religious orthodoxy [in a film about the crucifixion]. The historical lesson here is that absolute moralism when mixed with politics not only produces zealots who believe they have a monopoly on the truth and a legitimate rationale for refusing to engage ambiguities, it also fuels an intolerance towards others who do not follow the scripted, righteous path of officially sanctioned beliefs and behavior. Family values is now joined with an *emotionally charged rhetorical* appeal to faith as the new code words for cultural conservatism. As right-wing religion conjoins with political ideology and political power, it not only legitimates intolerance and anti-democratic forms of religious correctness, it also lays the groundwork for a growing authoritarianism which easily derides appeals to reason, dissent, dialogue, and secular humanism. How else to explain the growing number of Christian conservative educators who want to impose the teaching of creationism in the schools, ban sex education from the curricula, and subordinate scientific facts to religious dogma.

With George W. Bush's mandate to govern for four more years, religious correctness appears to be exercising a powerful influence on American society. The morality police seem to be everywhere denouncing everything from Janet Jackson's out of wardrobe display [where she showed a bare breast at a Superbowl halftime show] to the wanton Satanic influence of the television show *Desperate Housewives*. But the morality police do more than censor and impose their theocratic moralism on everyone else's behavior, they also elect politicians, and this does not augur well for the future of democracy in the United States. The rise of the religious zealot as politician is readily apparent not only in high profile religious hucksters such as [former U.S. Attorney General] John Ashcroft and the current "chosen" occupant of the White House, but also in the emergence of a new breed of faith-bearing politicians being elected to the highest level of government—readily supported by a media largely controlled by conservative corporate interests and a growing evangelical base of Christian fundamentalists. Conservative Christian moralism now travels straight to the *highest levels* of power as can be seen in the recent election of a new crop of "opportunistic ayatollahs on the right" to the U.S. Senate. For instance, the newly elected senator from Oklahoma, Tom Coburn, has not only publicly argued for the death penalty for doctors who perform abortions, he has also insisted that lesbianism is so rampart in the schools in Oklahoma that school officials only let one girl go at a time to the bathroom. Jim DeMint, the new senator from South Carolina, stated that he would not want to see "a single woman who was pregnant and living with her boyfriend" teaching in the public schools. He has also argued that he wants to ban gays from teaching in public schools as well. Jon Thune, the newly elected senator from South Dakota, supports a constitutional amendment banning flag burning, not to mention making permanent Bush's tax cuts for the rich.

## Bush As God's President

Widely recognized as creating the first faith-based presidency, George W. Bush has done more during his first term to advance the agenda of right-wing evangelicals than any other president in recent history, and he will continue to do so in his second term. What is most disturbing is not simply that many of his religious supporters believe that Bush is their leader but that he is also embraced as a "messenger from God," whose job it is to implement God's will. For example, Bob Jones III, the president of a fundamentalist college of the same name, argued in a written letter to President Bush: "Christ has allowed you to be his servant" in order to "leave an imprint for righteousness. . . . In your re-election, God has graciously granted America—though she doesn't deserve it—a reprieve from the agenda of paganism. You have been given a mandate. We the people expect your voice to be like the clear and certain sound of a trumpet. . . . Don't equivocate. Put your agenda on the front burner and let it boil. You owe the liberals nothing. They despise you because they despise your Christ." Jones goes on to claim that since "Christ has allowed [Bush] to be His servant in this nation . . . you will have the opportunity to appoint many conservative judges and exercise forceful leadership with the congress in passing legislation that is defined by biblical norm regarding the family, sexuality, sanctity of life, religious freedom, freedom of speech, and limited government." This is more than a call by Christian social conservatives and "power puritans," as [columnist] Maureen Dowd calls them, to appoint conservative judges, prevent homosexuals from securing jobs as teachers, and approve legislation that would stop stem cell research and eliminate the reproductive rights of women; it is also an example of the "bloodthirsty feelings of revenge" that now motivate many of Bush's religious boosters.

The ideological fervor, if not call for vengeance, that drives many of Bush's Christian fundamentalist supporters is also evident in the words of Bush supporter Hardy Billington who states, "To me, I just believe God controls everything, and God uses the president to keep evil down, to see the darkness and protect this nation. Other people will not protect us. God gives people choices to make. God gave us this president to be the man to protect the nation at this time." Bush seems to harbor the same arrogant illusion and out of that illusion has emerged a government that pushes aside self-criticism, uncertainty, and doubt in favor of a faith-based certainty and moral righteousness bereft of critical reflection. In fact, fear, slander, and God were the cornerstone of the Bush 2004 presidential campaign. First, [Vice President Dick] Cheney argued that if [Democratic presidential candidate John] Kerry were elected, it would mean the country would be subjected to terrorist attacks, which amounted to "Vote Bush or Die." Second, the Swift Boat Campaign successfully led the American people to believe that Kerry was a coward rather than a war hero, in spite of the five medals he won in Vietnam. And, finally, God became the ultimate referent to mobilize millions of additional votes from Christian fundamentalists. Matthew Rothschild, the editor of *The Progressive*, points out that the Republicans sent out pieces of literature in Arkansas and West Virginia "claiming the Democrats were going to take everyone's Bibles away. . . . On the front of one such envelope, sent from the Republican National Committee, was a picture of a Bible with the word 'BANNED' slapped across it. 'This will be Arkansas . . . if you don't vote,' it said." It appears that the high-pitched righteousness proclaimed by Bush's evangelical army of supporters took a vacation in order to play dirty politics during the Bush/Kerry campaign.

## Anti-Intellectualism

[Writer] Ron Suskind has argued that the one key feature of Bush's faith-based presidency is that it scorns "open dialogue,

Don Addis. Reproduced by permission.

based on facts, [which] is not seen as something of inherent value." Jim Wallis, a progressive evangelical pastor who was called upon by Bush to bring together a range of clergy to talk about faith and poverty, discovered rather quickly that Bush was not open to inconvenient facts or ideas at odds with what Bush often refers to as "his instincts." Wallis claims that as he got to work over time with Bush in the White House what he "started to see at this point was the man that would emerge over the next year—a messianic American Calvinist. He doesn't want to hear from anyone who doubts him." Bush became widely recognized as a President that exhibited a dislike, if not disdain, for contemplation, examining the facts, or dealing with friendly queries about the reasons for his decisions.

Rampant anti-intellectualism coupled with Taliban-like[1] moralism now boldly translates into everyday cultural practices as right-wing evangelicals live out their messianic

1. The Taliban was a fundamentalist group that governed Afghanistan before the U.S. invasion in fall 2001.

view of the world. For instance, more and more conservative pharmacists are refusing to fill prescriptions for religious reasons. Mixing medicine, politics, and religion means that some women are being denied birth control pills or any other product designed to prevent conception. It gets worse. Bush's much exalted religious fundamentalism does more than promote a disdain for critical thought and reinforce retrograde forms of homophobia and patriarchy; it also inspires an aggressive militarism, wrapped up in the language of a holy war. One telling example can be found in a story recently announced by *Agence France-Presse*. It reported that a group of evangelical marines prepared to "battle barbarians" before their assault on Fallujah in Iraq by listening to heavy metal-flavored lyrics in praise of Christ while a "female voice cried out on the loudspeakers 'You are the sovereign, Your name is holy. You are the pure spotless lamb.'" Just before the battle, a chaplain had the soldiers line up in order to dab their heads with oil, while he told them "God's people would be anointed with oil." It now appears that Bush's war for "democracy" is defined by many of his followers as a "holy war" against infidels. . . .

Authoritarianism takes many forms and its most recent expression appears to be gaining ground through the relentless force of a moral values crusade at home and abroad. Needless to say, cultural politics is alive and well in the United States, but it has to be reinvented so as to serve democracy rather than shut it down. What is at stake here is the challenge of rethinking the meaning of politics for the twenty-first century. This is a challenge that cannot be left to the "My God's Better Than Yours" crowd, who disavow democratic values for a politics of "Horns and Halos."

> "Evangelical Christians, more than any
> other group today, are responsible for
> America being a godly country."

# Christian Fundamentalism Promotes Moral Government in the United States

### Shmuley Boteach

*Rabbi Shmuley Boteach argues in this viewpoint that Americans reelected President George W. Bush because they wanted a Christian president who would promote morality in government. He contends that evangelical Christians are a positive political force because they insist that government help the poor, protect the persecuted, and promote freedom. Boteach also praises evangelical Christians for helping shield children from the corrosive influence of American pop culture. Boteach is a nationally syndicated radio host and a best-selling author.*

As you read, consider the following questions:

1. According to the author, what did exit polls show was the most important issue to American voters in the 2004

Shmuley Boteach, "George Bush's America: Moral Beacon in a Dark World," Jewish Press.com, November 10, 2004. Reproduced by permission.

presidential election?

2. What voting block has, according to the author, revolutionized the way the world does business?

3. What are the views of evangelical Christians toward materialism, according to the author?

The American people have once again demonstrated that they are the most glorious on earth [by reelecting President George W. Bush in 2004].

The entire world ganged up on them to dump a moral president whose signature issue was a belief that people have a right to be free. Europe mobilized its millions in the streets to show their hatred of this man and his ideals. The UN [United Nations] frowned at his speeches and treated him with contempt. Hollywood and the recording industry unleashed its superstars to prevail upon the American people that they dare not reelect a monster. And [Islamic terrorist] Osama bin Laden released a video tape informing individual states that if they voted against Bush they would be free from terrorist attack.

In the end, even American Jews abandoned this steadfast friend of Israel and gave [Democratic candidate] John Kerry 75 percent of their votes.

Never in the history of the United States has more pressure been brought to bear on the American electorate to dump a leader whose values the world so loathed. But in the end, not the glamour of Hollywood, nor the threats of terrorists, nor the alienation of Europe, nor the condescension of the UN, could break the American people's commitment to a moral presidency.

With all the pressure in the world to become like the rest of the world—overlooking genocide and making deals with tyrants—the American people voted to retain a faith-based presidency, even if it meant going it alone. Exit polls showed that morality, even more than security, was the single biggest issue animating American voters.

## The Rise of the Moral Voter

The rise of the moral voter is an earthquake that has forever changed the American political landscape. Who would ever have seriously believed that morality would be the single biggest consideration for politicians? But there it is. Gone are the days when politicians can seek office merely by pandering to voters by promising them jobs, health care, and pork. Now, politicians who want to connect with the electorate will be forced to articulate a powerful moral vision of something worth fighting for. Bush did this with his constant focus on the fight for human freedom and his pledge to protect the family.

This election was never really about Bush, Kerry, or even Iraq. Nor was it a referendum on conservative verses liberal. Rather, it was a challenge to the very notion of whether faith-as-policy had any place in a modern, technologically-advanced republic. And the victory was not for a man and his followers but for a belief in right and wrong and how religious conviction must be first translated into protecting human life through a fight against tyranny and state-sponsored murder.

Those Bush supporters who gloat over the blow inflicted on Bush's opponents betray an arrogance which in turn betrays a lack of commitment to moral principles, thereby eroding the cause for which the victory was sought. [Liberals] Michael Moore and Al Gore can rant all they like that Bush is a religious fraud, that he went into Iraq for oil and power rather than security and humanitarian concerns. Why vindicate their meanspiritedness with a meanspiritedness of our own? Why trivialize a moral victory by making it a personal victory?

Right and wrong does not belong to President Bush or any of the people who voted for him, but is rather the eternal inheritance of all of God's children, and in that sense, even those who voted against Bush share in his victory.

I am well aware that many Americans approach the increasing religiosity and moral commitment of the body politic with foreboding. They fear a theocracy that will be oppressive and infringe upon their rights. It is for Bush supporters to refute this unjust fear by demonstrating not only magnanimity in victory but a deep commitment to harmony and unity.

In behaving modestly in victory, Bush's supporters have no better example than President Bush himself. Many things have impressed me about this president over the past few years, but perhaps none more so than his refusal to respond in kind to those who called him a liar and compared him to Hitler. Here was the most powerful man on earth who consistently ignored the savage attacks on his character and instead went humbly on with his work. The American people have rewarded this humility with a considerable mandate which I trust he will continue to use over the next four years to fight evil and pursue justice. . . .

## A Faith-Based Presidency

Although they have become the most hated nation on earth for doing so, Americans chose another four years of a faith-based presidency and were happy to continue with their pariah president, even if that meant being rejected by the international community for their commitment to a moral foreign policy.

If only Israelis would follow their close ally's example and behave more like a chosen nation themselves. Unfortunately, the United States and Israel could not be headed in more different directions.

President Bush's stunning victory was a mandate from the people for a more moral nation. The contrast with Israel could not be more stark; an Israeli prime minister speaking about God is the certain kiss of electoral death.

## The Safest People on the Planet

The reality is that Christians, as a group, are the safest, most responsible and law abiding people on this planet. True Christians are about as dangerous to society as an arsonist with an empty matchbook. Or the French army.

Why doesn't that matter?

So demonized are Christians that any time one is mentioned in the public forum, the term itself is usually preceded by unflattering adjectives, like "right-wing," "zealous," and the *F*-word—"fundamentalist."

*Jon Dougherty, "Christians Are No Danger,"*
*World Net Daily.com,*
*June 28, 2000. www.wnd.com.*

Most Americans would find it shocking that the political leaders of the Jewish nation, who gifted the Creator to the world, would never consider mentioning G-d for fear of alienating a majority secular electorate who are deeply distrustful of faith. In this respect, Israeli leaders are more like European leaders who are about as likely to invoke the name of God as they are the name of Zeus.

Then there is the fact that the majority of Americans just don't care about being cut off from the rest of the world. In this election the American people made a resounding judgment: If America is right and the world is wrong, we will show them our contempt.

John Kerry's central campaign platform was the need to rebuild frayed alliances with Europe and the UN that he said were damaged by Bush administration "arrogance." In the end, Americans decided that their strength lay not in being popular but in being moral. . . .

## Evangelicals Made America Godly

The impact the American evangelical voting bloc has had on world affairs is incalculable and explains why there has been a revolution in the way the world does business. The staunch support of evangelical Christians has enabled George W. Bush to pursue a foreign policy based not on expediency or *realpolitik,* but on a deep-seated morality wherein tyrants are punished and the oppressed liberated. These policies would have been unthinkable without the steadfast support of Bush's die-hard constituency of evangelical Christians who comprise one-quarter of the American electorate.

I am a Jew who is deeply in love with evangelical Christians. Although I am at odds with them on various issues, they today constitute the most potent force for good in America, and the most influential constituency who consistently demands that America be a nation of justice, standing up for the persecuted and living up to its founding ideals of serving as a global beacon of freedom.

To be sure, I am devoted to Judaism. Wild horses and iron combs could never pry me away from my Jewish identity and I have devoted my life to the dissemination of Jewish ideas in the mainstream culture and to bringing wayward Jews back to their heritage. But I must give credit where credit is due. And evangelical Christians, more than any other group today, are responsible for America being a godly country.

Whenever I am in the company of evangelical Christians, I feel completely at home, among true brothers and sisters of faith. More so, I feel inspired. When evangelical Christians talk to me about God, they speak with an immediacy and sense of intimacy which is both inspiring and impressive. To the evangelicals, God is a loving father rather than a distant relative. And unlike secularists who love making up their own morality, evangelical Christians humbly submit to the Divine Will. The potency of evangelical faith is manifest in their being at the forefront of feeding the hungry, curing the sick, and giving clothing to the poor.

Unlike so many Americans, evangelical Christians utterly reject materialism. They raise godly children who are open-hearted and uncorrupted. Evangelical Christian parents protect their children from a corrosive culture that is so harmful to America's youth. The evangelicals have created their own music, TV and film industries which promote values-based entertainment as opposed to crude sexual exploitation. Their women are taught to value themselves and would never contemplate surrendering their bodies to a man who has not committed to them in marriage. And their men are taught to value women and to work to be worthy of them.

This is not to say I don't have serious disagreements with evangelicals. It is on the subject of Jesus, especially, and other related theological questions, that I am, of course, most distant from my evangelical brothers and sisters. I have had many televised debates against leading evangelicals forcefully rejecting Jesus as the Jewish messiah. But for all that, I have never felt any emotional distance from the evangelicals.

## Christians Are More Compassionate

Many of my Jewish brethren reject evangelical Christians as dogmatic and intolerant. In so doing they are guilty of themselves of rejecting one of Judaism's most seminal teachings: to judge a man by his actions rather than his beliefs. Just try to find kinder, more compassionate people who are more willing to assist their fellow man in a time of crisis, than the evangelicals. And this is especially true of the evangelical love for Israel.

As an American Jew, I have two great loves: the United States and Israel. The Talmud says that what makes Israel unique is that God's presence is a tangible reality in the Holy Land. In Israel, one can sense and feel God's holy presence. Thanks largely to evangelical Christians, the same is true today of the United States. God is alive and well in America. And it is primarily for that reason that this great country is so blessed.

> *Hindu "police . . . participated directly in the burning and looting of Muslim shops and homes and the killing and mutilation of Muslims."*

# Hindu Fundamentalism Threatens India

**Amitabh Pal**

*In this viewpoint Amitabh Pal argues that Hindu fundamentalist violence in India is carried out against non-Hindus with the collusion of India's government. The United States does not criticize the violence, says Pal, because India cooperates in its war on terror and is important to U.S. business interests. Pal says Hindu voters support the fundamentalists in sufficient numbers so that more violence is likely in the future. Pal is managing editor of the* Progessive *magazine.*

As you read, consider the following questions:

1. According to sources cited by the author, what reason did National Security Adviser Condoleezza Rice give for not criticizing the violence described in the article?

2. What U.S. business interests in India are mentioned by

Amitabh Pal, "Bush Ignores India's Pogrom," *The Progressive*, July 1, 2003. Copyright © 2003 by The Progressive, Inc. Reproduced by permission of *The Progressive*.

the author as important?

3. What did the Human Rights Report say, as cited by Pal?

I visited [non-violence advocate Mahatma] Gandhi's home state of Gujarat in mid-December for my brother-in-law's wedding. Coincidentally, it was the day of elections to decide the fate of a right-wing state government. According to Human Rights Watch, that government was complicit in the massacre of at least 2,000 Muslims early last year [2002], the highest toll in Hindu-Muslim violence since India's independence.

The election results caused my stomach to churn. The Bharatiya Janata Party (BJP) government headed by Chief Minister Narendra Modi returned to power. It successfully capitalized on Hindu animosity toward Muslims and harped on local pride, claiming to defend the honor of the state against attacks by secularist outsiders. Gandhi wouldn't have been too happy.

## Right-wing Hindu Fundamentalism

The events in Gujarat are only the most obvious expression of how the growth of right-wing Hindu fundamentalism since the late 1980s has undermined Gandhi's legacy. This trend is not just confined to Gandhi's home state. A coalition headed by the BJP, the same party that governs Gujarat, currently governs all of India.

The United States has been, at best, equivocal in its response to the Gujarat anti-Muslim campaign. And it has been half-hearted in trying to stem the flow of funds from the United States to Hindu extremist groups in India.

The BJP's militant, hard-line attitude apparently does not trouble the Bush Administration, which has drawn closer since [the September 11, 2001, terrorist attacks] to the Indian government (even while maintaining an alliance with the BJP'S bugbear, General Pervez Musharraf's regime in Pakistan). The BJP has used the post-September 11 climate as a cover for harsh internal measures, such as passing stiff anti-terrorism laws and, as Gujarat shows, targeting Muslims. The Indian government has reciprocated U.S. friendship by strongly supporting the Bush Administration's campaign in Afghanistan and by being reticent about the Iraq War.

According to *The New York Times*, the only public remarks about Gujarat that the U.S. ambassador, Robert Blackwill, made in the aftermath of the violence was: "All our hearts go out to the people who were affected by this tragedy. I don't have anything more to say than that." In contrast, after terrorists killed twenty-four Kashmiris in late March this year, Blackwill was quick to issue a statement condemning "the ghastly murder of innocent men, women, and children." Blackwill did not even visit Gujarat subsequent to the pogrom.

## U.S. Officials Ignore the Problem

[Former] National Security Adviser Condoleezza Rice was asked by *The Hindu*, a leading national paper, about "why the United States has not been forthcoming in its criticism." She responded that the BJP "government is leading India well, and it will do the right thing."

Assistant Secretary of State for South Asian Affairs Christina Rocca did term the events in Gujarat "really horrible," but she neglected to assign any blame.

When [Former] Secretary of State Colin Powell visited India last July, he made no mention of Gujarat, as Mira Kamdar pointed out in *World Policy Journal*. The furthest that the Bush Administration went was to raise the matter privately with the Indian government, warning that it was harming India's image, according to the Bombay-based *Economic Times*. By contrast, the European Union likened the Gujarat situation to apartheid and said that it had similarities with Nazi Germany of the 1930s. Apparently, the U.S. government has deemed it more important to keep India on its side in the "war on terrorism" than to risk a row over even grotesque human rights violations.

The state-sponsored violence in Gujarat came in retaliation for the actions of a Muslim mob, which, on February 27 last year, burned alive nearly sixty Hindus on a train in the city of Godhra. The train was returning from Ayodhya in Northern India, where many of the train's occupants had gone as part of a mobilization to build a temple to Lord Ram, a Hindu deity, on the site of a mosque. The retaliation against Muslims started the next morning, with the worst incidents happening over the next three days. In addition to those killed, the violence forced more than 100,000 Muslims into becoming refugees and destroyed 360 Muslim places of worship. Numerous women were raped, sometimes gang-raped. "I have never known a riot which has used the sexual subjugation of women so widely as an instrument of violence as the recent barbarity in Gujarat," wrote Harsh Mander, a government official who resigned in disgust. "This was not a riot," one senior police official told *The New York Times*. "It was a state-sponsored pogrom."

India's National Human Rights Commission faulted the state government for "failure of intelligence and action." The commission named senior BJP officials as among the accused. "These are grave matters, indeed, that must not be allowed to be forgiven or forgotten," the commission said.

## The Police Participate

Human Rights Watch issued a report on the massacres, entitled "We Have No Orders to Save You." It detailed the extensive complicity of the authorities in the violence. "In many cases, the police led the charge, using gunfire to kill Muslims who got in the mobs' way," the report states. "A key BJP state minister is reported to have taken over police control rooms in Ahmedabad on the first day of the carnage, issuing orders to disregard pleas for assistance from Muslims." Police also "participated directly in the burning and looting of Muslim shops and homes and the killing and mutilation of Muslims. In many cases, under the guise of offering assistance, the police led the victims directly into the hands of their killers."

Ahsan Jafri, a former member of parliament, lived in the Gulmarg Society neighborhood in Ahmedabad, the largest city in Gujarat and the site of the worst violence. Jafri tried to use his home as a shelter for Muslims. But then a Hindu mob approached his house.

"On February 28, we went to Ahsan Jafri's home for safety," says Mehboob Mansoori, in testimony to Human Rights Watch. Jafri "was holding the door closed. Then the door broke down. They pulled him out and hit him with a sword across the forehead, then across the stomach, then on his legs. . . . They then took him on the road, poured kerosene on him, and burned him. There was no police at all."

Mansoori managed to survive. However, his family was all but wiped out. "Eighteen people from my family died," he told Human Rights Watch. "All the women died. My brother, my three sons, one girl, my wife's mother, they all died. . . . Other girls were raped, cut, and burned. . . . Sixty-five to seventy people were killed inside."

Jafri's daughter, Nishrin Hussain, who lives in Delaware, remains outraged.

"It was prepared and preplanned with government blessing all along," she says. "The police and the government connived with the rioters."

After the riots, Nishrin returned to Gujarat to see what happened. She was not welcome. During her visit, people circulated posters that contained veiled threats on her life, she says. And when she went to one village, a mob told her if she dared to come back, she'd be killed.

The U.S. Commission on International Religious Freedom, a body set up by Congress, denounced the violence in Gujarat and has even named India as a "country of particular concern," thus placing it in the company of such nations as China, Saudi Arabia, and Burma. Under the International Religious Freedom Act of 1998, the President is required to take diplomatic or economic actions against countries on the list.

## U.S. Silence

Felice D. Gaer, chair of the commission, is critical of the Bush Administration's response to the Gujarat violence. "There's been no public comment by the Administration on Gujarat other than in response to a direct question," Gaer says. "The ambassador hasn't visited the region. Senior officials are not interested in holding anyone responsible for the violence."

Assistant Secretary of State Rocca claimed on March 22 at a Senate hearing on South Asia that "much action" has been taken by the Indian government. "The legal system in India is agonizingly slow and that gives the impression that nothing is happening," she said. "But the fact of the matter is that they did take action and they are continuing to take action," she said. The "United States has spoken out loudly and often on the terrible events of Gujarat, and it did not in any way get a pass from anywhere in the world, much less from the Bush Administration."

Sunil Lal, press officer at the Indian Embassy in Washington, is happy with the Bush Administration's approach to Gujarat. "The U.S. Administration is aware of the efforts made by the government of India, and you must have heard Christina Rocca's recent testimony on this subject," he says.

Others rebut the State Department's claims. As Smita Narula of Human Rights Watch pointed out in an op-ed in *The Asian Wall Street Journal* on the first anniversary of the pogrom, "There have been no convictions of those responsible." In contrast, the government charged 131 Muslims under the harsh Prevention of Terrorism Act for the train burning. Between July and October, the government closed the Muslim refugee camps.

## Still Roaming Free

Perpetrators of the demolition of the Babri [Muslim] mosque in Ayodhya, Uttar Pradesh [India], are still roaming free 13 years later. The inquiry into the violence has yet to present its findings; as for the suspects, formal charges have been filed against them and that is all.

On 6 December 1992, extremist Hindus demolished the mosque of Babri Masjid (XVI century), which was constructed, according to them, on the birthplace of the god Ram.

*Nirmala Carvalho, "Perpetrators of Ayodhya Violence Scot-free After 13 Years," AsiaNews.it, December 10, 2005 www.asianews.it.*

The response in the U.S. Congress was also, for the most part, mild. Jim McDermott, a liberal Democrat from Washington, spoke very carefully about Gujarat last April before an audience of Indian Americans in an event co-sponsored by the Overseas Friends of Bharatiya Janata Party. He said that while some members of Congress were concerned about the situation, he appreciated the Indian government's response.

"Prime Minister Vajpayee has done a remarkable job in trying to balance the forces that make up a country as diverse as India," he said. McDermott was, however, more critical of the BJP in a phone interview, saying the party was "wrong to inject religion into politics" and that this "just won't work."

## Financial Clout

The lack of a stronger response may be due to the increasing visibility and financial clout of the prosperous Indian American community, currently 1.7 million in number, with Gujaratis comprising 40 percent of the total. "Intensive lobbying by members of the Indian American community prevented introduction of a resolution in the U.S. Congress condemning the violence," states Human Rights Watch. In the 2000 election cycle, Indian Americans contributed at least $13 million, according to Federal Election Commission data. Plus, growing U.S. business interests in India (notably in software, telemarketing, and the arms industry) have fostered a pro-India climate on the Hill. As a result, about 130 members of Congress are members of the Congressional Caucus on India and Indian Americans. McDermott is a past chair of the caucus. Congressmen Frank Pallone, Democrat of New Jersey, and Gary Ackerman, Democrat of New York, both founders of the caucus, were last year awarded the Padma Bhushan, a top Indian civilian honor.

Senator Joseph Biden, Democrat of Delaware, and Senator Thomas Carper, Democrat of Delaware, have been more outspoken. They called up family members of the murdered ex-parliamentarian, Ahsan Jafri, to express their sympathy. Biden also addressed the issue publicly, saying that the killings were "just plain wrong" and that "nothing justifies the slaughter of innocent women and children." "About 2,000 people have been slaughtered in mob violence there, often— whether you like to hear it or not—with the collusion of local officials," he said at a conference hosted by an Indian business group.

But Biden took some heat for his stance from members of the Indian American community. "The very next day, his office was bombarded with calls and e-mails saying, 'You stay out of this; this is an internal Indian matter.' He backed off," says Najid Hussain, Jafri's son-in-law.

Funds from charities in the United States flow to Hindu extremist groups in India, some of which may have been involved in the Gujarat violence. The Bush Administration has done little about this, in marked contrast to its vigorous attempts to investigate money allegedly going to Al Qaeda.

Vijay Prashad, author of *The Karma of Brown Folk*, a study of the Indian diaspora, estimates that Hindu extremist groups in this country raise at least $10 million a year, of which perhaps 10 percent goes to India.

One of the most notable Indian charitable organizations in the United States is the India Development and Relief Fund, which, according to *The Financial Times*, raised more than $10 million between 1997 and 2001 and sent $3.2 million to India between 1994 and 2000.

## Calls to Stop the Hate

An ad hoc coalition of Indian Americans, the Campaign to Stop Funding Hate, issued a report a few months ago alleging that the relief fund supports Hindu hate groups in India. One of these groups is the Vanvasi Kalyan Parishad (Tribals Welfare Organization), says Shalini Gera, a spokesperson for the campaign. The organization was involved in anti-Christian violence in the late 1990s in Gujarat, according to *The Times of India*, and in the anti-Muslim campaign, according to *Frontline* magazine. The Vanvasi Kalyan Parishad "directed violence against Muslims" during the Gujarat killings, reports *Frontline*. (Attempts to reach the organization for comment were unsuccessful.)

*The Financial Times* reports that the Justice Department may be investigating the fund. Vinod Prakash, the founder and president of the India Development and Relief Fund (IDRF), vehemently denies that his organization has received any sort of communication from the Bush Administration.

"It will prove to be an uphill battle for the U.S. to properly investigate and scrutinize these organizations because of their links to India's ruling party, the BJP," says Narula of Human Rights Watch in *The Financial Times*. "The U.S. needs India as an ally right now."

Prakash also says that his organization doesn't fund any Hindu right-wing groups, such as the Vanvasi Kalyan Parishad. (The website of the group does name Vanvasi Kalyan Parishad among the list of "IDRF-supported groups in Gujarat.") He does not, however, deny ideological affiliations. "I have every right as a person to be close to this or that organization," he says. "But the IDRF has never discriminated. As a proud Hindu, I will never discriminate in my humanitarian service."

By the time the Gujarat election results were announced, I had left the state. But I was appalled by the reaction I was hearing from Hindus in other parts of the country. While some opposed the Modi government, others were unabashedly supportive, and a whole lot of people were ambivalent. It is this reaction—both inside India and outside—that the BJP is counting on to forge ahead with its sectarian and violent agenda for the country.

"The Bush Administration and Congress should tell the Indian government that justice must be done," says Najid Hussain. "The propagation of such an ideology has to stop."

*"A pluralistic country like India needs secularism like its life-blood. India has been pluralist not since post-modern times but for centuries."*

# Hindu Fundamentalism Will Not Seriously Threaten India

## Ashgar Ali Engineer

*In this viewpoint Ashgar Ali Engineer argues that the leaders of India's independence movement recognized that India must be a secular democracy because of its religious diversity. All religions must be recognized and protected in such a nation, they believed. Though Hindu fundamentalism has grown in India, the author says secularism will prevail as India's leaders foresaw. Because democracy in India is strong, secularism will grow, thereby quashing the forces of religious fundamentalism, Engineer maintains. Engineer established the Center for Study of Society and Secularism in Mumbai, India, and has authored more than forty-seven books.*

As you read, consider the following questions:

1. According to the author, which is more aggressive in

Asghar Ali Engineer, "Future of Secularism in India," *Secular Perspective*, August 16-31, 2003. Reproduced by permission.

India, Hindu fundamentalism or Islamic fundamentalism?

2. Did India's education system cultivate a secular outlook, according to the author?

3. Does the author believe Hindu fundamentalists will stop promoting Hindu nationalism in the near future?

The question of the future of secularism in India is very important, particularly at this juncture. The fundamentalist forces are raising their head in India as in other countries of the world. No religion is exception to this. There are many reasons for this. In India, Hindu fundamentalism has become much more aggressive than, say, Muslim fundamentalism. Secularism today is in much greater danger than ever before due to Hindutva[1] militancy.

Secularism is highly necessary if India wants to survive as a nation. But apart from survival of Indian nationalism and Indian unity, secularism is necessary for modern democratic polity. And this need for secular polity becomes much greater if the country happens to be as diverse and plural as India. Secularism is a great need for democratic pluralism. . . .

## Roots of Indian Secularism

Our leaders and freedom fighters were well aware of the need for a secular and modern democratic polity for India. They also knew that India is a highly religious country and that secularism in the sense of hostility or indifference to religion will never be acceptable to the people of India. Secularism was never meant to be indifference to religion by India's leaders. It is for this reason that even the most orthodox among Hindus and Muslims accepted it as a viable ideology for Indian unity and integrity. . . .

---

1. Hindutva is a Hindu nationalist movement.

[Jawaharla] Nehru,[2] though personally agnostic, never imposed agnostic or atheistic secularism. He was too much of a democrat to attempt that. He said in his answer to a query by an Indian student at Oxford University in the fifties that in the U.K. state has a religion (Anglican Christianity) but people of England are quite indifferent to religion, but in India the state has no religion but people are very religious. Therefore, in the Indian situation secularism means equal protection to all religions.

Nehru was greatly committed, more than anyone else in post-independence India, to the concept of secularism. He never compromised on this question. He was well aware of the fact that secularism is a great cementing force for the diverse people of India. He, as an idealist, thought that with the spread of modern scientific and technological education secularism would spread and find greater and greater acceptability. However, not only it did not happen that way but [religious] communalism and obscurantism spread with more intensity than secularism. . . .

## Religious History

There are several reasons for this, all of which we cannot analyse here. Some of them of course must be mentioned. Very few people in the Congress [Party][3] were as genuinely committed to secularism as Nehru. Many eminent Congress leaders were opposed to it in their heart of hearts. They tried to sabotage the Nehruvian vision in his own lifetime and they became much more active after his death. Nehru could not pay much attention to the educational system in his lifetime. It could not be reformed. The old textbooks with the communal approach introduced during the British period were never changed. The Congress leaders themselves approved of

2. Nehru was a leader of India's movement for independence from Great Britain, and India's first prime minister.
3. The Indian National Congress Party was led by Nehru.

---

## Secularism Defeats Fundamentalism

[In May of 2004] India, the world's largest democracy, voted decisively for secularism, not religious fundamentalism. . . . Indian voters handed the "Secular Front" (now renamed "United Progressive Alliance") led by the Congress Party a landslide electoral victory and dashed the Hindu right's hopes of winning another term as a parliamentary majority.

The gains of the Secular Front are remarkable. Congress—the party of Mohandas K. Gandhi and Jawaharlal Nehru—and its allies won 216 seats in the 539-seat Lok Sabha (parliament).

These elections were historic. In election campaigns nationwide, contentious issues were raised, foremost among which was secularism versus religious fundamentalism. Secularism and people's power won the day.

*Francis Gonsalves*, National Catholic Reporter,
*May 28, 2004.*

---

them. Those who did not, could not show enough courage to demand essential changes in history textbooks. Thus most of the Indians grew with subtle or pronounced communal mindset.

In fact the educated were thus more affected with the communal virus than the illiterate masses who never studied in schools and colleges. Similarly urban areas were more affected with communal virus than rural areas. Formation of Pakistan also greatly affected the thinking of the educated middle class Hindus and they looked upon Muslims as responsible for the creation of Pakistan. They were never taught the complex political factors which brought about the existence of Pakistan and that it was a small percentage of elite Muslims who were more responsible for the creation of Pakistan than the Muslim masses who did not even migrate to that country. . . .

Thus the education system did not cultivate a secular outlook, and a conservative political outlook continued to strengthen the communal mindset among the educated middle classes. The Muslim leaders in independent India . . . could not provide moderate and wise leadership to Muslim masses. They also remained not only extremely cautious in their approach but never prepared Muslim masses for a modern secular polity in India. They were more insistent on minority rights than on the necessity for change.

This attitude was further strengthened among these leaders due to frequent occurrences of communal riots. The Jabalpur riot of 1961 shook Nehru as much as Indian Muslims to the core. For the first time they became greatly apprehensive of their security and began to withdraw in their shell. This further reinforced conservatism and set up another hurdle in developing a secular outlook among the Muslims. The Jabalpur riots were followed by more intense communal violence in Ahmedabad in 1969 and Bhivandi-Jalgaon in 1970.[4]

The end of seventies and early eighties witnessed a number of major communal riots in which hundreds were killed brutally. . . . [P]ropaganda, on the other hand, was bringing more and more Hindus in the fold of Hindutva. All these developments were a sure prescription for increasingly weakening secular forces in the country. . . .

The decade of the eighties saw a rise of religious militancy among Hindus, Sikhs[5] and Muslims. This decade also witnessed horrendous communal violence in North India. . . .

And in the beginning of the nineties the [Islamic Mosque] Babri Masjid was demolished [by militant Hindus] which

4. The Jabalpur, Ahmedabad, and Bhivandi-Jalgaon riots involved religious conflict.

5. Sikhs are another religious minority in India.

pushed Indian secularism to the brink. It was the greatest disabler and was followed by Bombay riots, which shocked the whole world.

Thus we see Indian secularism has followed a tortuous course all through in the post-independence period. It is not surprising in an underdeveloped country like India with its immense poverty, insurmountable levels of unemployment and widespread illiteracy. The Bhartiya Janta Party (BJP), which came to power using its Hindutva card is not likely to give it up in the near future. With every election it intensifies its Hindutva agenda. The other members of the Sangh Parivar[6], specially the Vishva Hindu Parishad (VHP), tend to be more irresponsible as they do not have to govern. The VHP assumes extremist postures and threatens minorities. It is this irresponsible extremism which resulted in the Gujarat carnage which again shook the world. . . .

## Democracy Requires Secularism

In the given political circumstances the future of secularism does not seem to be bright. However, one should not take a short-term view based only on the given context. Human beings have always struggled to transcend their given situation. A purely contextual view tends to be realistic but also a restricted one. A vision, on the other hand, may not always be realistic but has a much broader sweep. And it is this broader sweep which shapes new realities and these new realities enable us to shape our future.

Though religion will never cease to be a force in human life, secularism will not lose its relevance either. The modern democratic polity cannot be sustained without the state being neutral to all religions or equally protective for all religions as Nehru put it. And it is in this sense that secularism in India will become more and more relevant. It should also be noted

6. Sangh Parivar is an affiliation of organizations promoting Hindutva.

that we should not pose secularism and religious orthodoxy as binary opposites, as some rationalists tend to do.

Faith will always remain an important component of human behaviour and there will always remain an element of orthodoxy in faith behaviour. Rational faith is certainly not an impossibility but it tends to be an elitist phenomenon. On the level of masses orthodoxy reigns rather than rationality, even in advanced societies. Also, economic advancement and reduction in levels of poverty and illiteracy will ultimately sideline communal bigotry and enhance the forces of secularism. Religious orthodoxy, unless challenged by the other's threats, would not yield to communalism. There is a *Laxman Rekha*[7] between religious orthodoxy and communal discourse.

India has stupendous challenges to meet due to its economic backwardness and unemployment, which sharpen communal tendencies. Unemployed and frustrated youth can easily be induced to think and act communally, as an unemployed youth tends to think that his unemployment is due more to his caste or community than economic backwardness. Thus chances of secularism will certainly brighten with more economic progress and reduced levels of unemployment, particularly educated unemployment.

Indian democracy, which is here to stay, is in itself a guarantee for the future of secularism. A pluralist country like India needs secularism like its life-blood. India has been pluralist not since post-modern times but for centuries and no one can wish away its bewildering pluralism, which can be sustained only with a religiously neutral polity. India has been passing through a very critical phase now but there is nothing to despair. The present communal turmoil is not here to stay. It would certainly yield to a more stable secular polity.

7. *Laxman Rekha* means "limit that cannot be crossed."

# Israeli Jewish Fundamentalists Promote Violence in the Middle East

*David Hirst*

*David Hirst argues in the following viewpoint that Jewish fundamentalists seek to replace democracy in Israel with religious rule. Under such rule, says Hirst, Arabs would not be entitled to equal rights and eventually would have to leave or be annihilated. Moreover, Jewish fundamentalists' beliefs, he says, obligate them to actively sabotage any American-sponsored peaceful settlement of the Arab-Israeli conflict. Hirst is a Middle East correspondent for the* Guardian *and author of* The Gun and the Olive Branch: The Roots of Violence in the Middle East.

As you read, consider the following questions:

"Cloaked in [fundamentalist Jewish] religion . . . destructive customary practices [in Israel] acquire a false patina of sanctity and become instruments of control."

1. What percentage of Israelis is fundamentalist, according to the author?

2. What obligation does Israel have to follow customary principles of morality, according to Jewish fundamentalists, as cited by the author?

3. What do Jewish fundamentalist leaders say is the divine mission of Israel?

Like its Islamic counterpart, Jewish fundamentalism in Israel has grown enormously in political importance over the past quarter-century. Its committed, hard-core adherents, as distinct from a larger body of the more traditionally religious, are thought to account for some 20 to 25 percent of the population. They, and more particularly the settlers among them, have acquired an influence, disproportionate to their numbers, over the whole Israeli political process, and especially in relation to the ultra-nationalist right, which, beneath its secular exterior, actually shares much of their febrile, exalted outlook on the world. It is fundamentalism of a very special, ethnocentric and fiercely xenophobic kind, with beliefs and practices that are "even more extremist," says [Israeli author and human rights activist Israel] Shahak, "than those attributed to the extremes of Islamic fundamentalism," if not "the most totalitarian system ever invented."

## Religious Law Will Replace Democracy

Like fundamentalism everywhere, the Jewish variety seeks to restore an ideal, imagined past. If it ever managed to do so, the Israel celebrated by the American "friends of Israel" as a "bastion of democracy in the Middle East" would, most assuredly, be no more. For, in its full and perfect form, the Jewish Kingdom that arose in its place would elevate a stern and wrathful God's sovereignty over any new-fangled, heathen concepts such as the people's will, civil liberties or human rights. It would be governed by the Halacha, or Jewish religious law, of which the rabbis would be the sole interpreters, and whose observance clerical commissars, installed in every public and private institution, would rigorously enforce, with the help of citizens legally obligated to report any offense to the authorities. A monarch, chosen by the rabbis, would rule and the Knesset [Israel's parliament] would be replaced by a Sanhedrin, or supreme judicial, ecclesiastic and administrative council. Men and women would be segregated in public, and "modesty" in female dress and conduct would be enforced by law. Adultery would be a capital offense, and anyone who drove on the Sabbath, or desecrated it in other ways, would be liable to death by stoning. As for non-Jews, the Halacha would be an edifice of systematic discrimination against them, in which every possible crime or sin committed by a Gentile against a Jew, from murder or adultery to robbery or fraud, would be far more heavily punished than the same crime or sin committed by a Jew against a Gentile—if, indeed, the latter were considered to be a felony at all, which it often would not be.

All forms of "idolatry or idol-worship," but especially Christian ones (for traditionally Muslims, who are not considered to be idolaters, are held in less contempt than Christians), would be "obliterated," in the words of Shas party leader Rabbi Ovadia Yossef. According to conditions laid down by Maimonides, whose Halacha rulings are holy writ to the fundamentalists, those Gentiles, or so-called "Sons of Noah," permitted to remain in the Kingdom could only do so as "resident aliens," obliged under law to accept the "inferiority" in perpetuity which that status entails, to "suffer the humiliation of servitude," and to be "kept down and not raise their heads to the Jews." At weekday prayers, the faithful would intone the special curse: "And may the apostates have no hope, and all the Christians perish instantly." One wonders what the Jerry Falwells and Pat Robertsons[1] think of all this; for it is strange, this new adoration by America's evangelicals of an

1. Falwell and Robertson are conservative Christian leaders.

Israel whose Jewish fundamentalists continue to harbor a doctrinal contempt for Christianity only rivaled by the contempt which the Christian fundamentalists reserve for the Jews themselves.

## The Messiah Is Coming

Fundamentalists come in a multitude of sects, often fiercely disputatious with one another on the finest and most esoteric points of doctrine, but all are agreed on this basic eschatological truth: It is upon the coming of the Messiah that the Jewish Kingdom will arise, and the twice-destroyed Temple will be reconstructed on the site where the [Islamic] Dome of the Rock and al-Aqsa mosques now stand. One school of fundamentalists, the Hanedim, believes that the Messiah will appear in His own good time, that the millennium, the End of Days, will come by the grace of God alone. The Shas party is their largest single political component. Their position has in it something of the traditional religious quietism, which, historically, opposed the whole idea of Zionism, immigration to Palestine and the establishment of a Jewish state.

The other school, less extreme in outward religious observances, is more so, indeed breathtakingly revolutionary, on one crucial point of dogma: the belief that the coming of the Messiah can be accomplished, or hastened, by human agency. In fact, the "messianic era" has already arrived. This messianic fundamentalism is represented by the National Religious Party, and its progeny, the settlers of the Gush Emunim, or Bloc of the Faithful, who eventually came to dominate it. Its adherents are ready to involve themselves in the world, sinful though it is, and, by so doing, they sanctify it. Except for the symbolic skullcap, they have adopted conventional modern dress; they include secular subjects in the curricula of their seminaries.

According to the teachings of their spiritual mentor, Rabbi Tzvi Yehuda Kook, the Gush, or at least the rabbis who lead it, are themselves the collective incarnation of the Messiah. Since, in biblical prophecy, the Messiah was to appear riding on an ass, he identified the ass as those errant, secular Jews who remain in stubborn ignorance of the exalted purpose of its divinely guided rider. In the shape of those early Zionists they had, it is true, performed the necessary task of carrying the Jews back to the Holy Land, settling it and founding a state there. But now they had served their historic purpose; now they had become obsolete in their failure to renounce their beastly, ass-like ways—and to perceive that Zionism has a divine, not merely a national, purpose.

## Israel Is Not Bound by Common Morality

The mainstream secular Zionist leadership had wanted the Jewish people to achieve "normality," to be as other peoples with a nation-state of their own. The messianics—and indeed, though for emotional more than doctrinal reasons, much of the nationalist right—hold that that is impossible; the Jews' "eternal uniqueness" stems from the covenant God made with them on Mount Sinai. So, as Rabbi Shlomo Aviner, a Gush leader and head of a yeshiva that studies the ancient priestly rites that would be revived if and when the Temple were rebuilt, put it, "while God requires other, normal nations to abide by abstract codes of 'justice and righteousness,' such laws do not apply to Jews." Since Zionism began, but especially since the 1967 war and Israel's conquest of the remainder of historic Palestine, the Jews have been living in a "transcendental political reality," or a state of "metaphysical transformation," one in which, through war and conquest, Israel liberates itself not only from its physical enemies, but from the "satanic" power which these enemies incarnate. The command to conquer the Land, says Aviner, is "above the moral, human considerations about the national rights of the Gentiles in our country." What he calls "messianic realism" dictates that Israel has been instructed to "be holy, not moral, and the general

## Jews Should Serve, Not Dominate Others

If you are a good Jew, you cannot be a Zionist [one working to establish a Jewish state in Palestine]. If you are a Zionist, you cannot be a good Jew. The reason for this is fairly simple to explain. The Jews are not a race, such as Caucausians or Negroes, as Hitler contended. The Jews are not a nation, like France, Great Britain, the United States, or any other of the nations. And they are not just a religion, like Catholicism, Buddhism, or any of the Protestant denominations. They are, rather, a unique combination, unlike any other. It is true that Jews are, according to the Bible and their own belief, the Chosen People. But they are not chosen for domination; they are not elected to rule over other people; but they are chosen for one purpose only: for service—to serve the Creator of the Universe and the Father of us all in a very special way, and thereby to serve all mankind.

*JewsNotZionists.org, "Judaism and Zionism, 1969."*
*www.jewsnotzionists.org.*

principles of morality, customary for all mankind, do not bind the people of Israel, because it has been chosen to be above them." It is not simply because the Arabs deem the land to be theirs that they resist this process—though, in truth, it is not theirs and they are simply "thieves" who took what always belonged to the Jews—it is because, as Gentiles, they are inherently bound to do so. "Arab hostility," says another Gush luminary, Rabbi Eliezer Waldman, director of the Kiryat Arba settlement's main yeshiva, "springs, like all anti-Semitism, from the world's recalcitrance" in the face of an Israel pursuing "its divine mission to serve as the heart of the world."

## Arabs Must Leave or Be Annihilated

So force is the only way to deal with the Palestinians. So long as they stay in the Land of Israel, they can only do so as "resident aliens" without "equality of human and civil rights," those being "a foreign democratic principle" that does not apply to them. But, in the end, they must leave. There are two ways in which that can happen. One is "enforced emigration." The other way is based on the biblical injunction to "annihilate the memory of Amalek." In an article on "The Command of Genocide in the Bible," Rabbi Israel Hess opined— without incurring any criticism from a state Rabbinate whose official duty it is to correct error wherever it finds it—that "the day will come when we shall all be called upon to wage this war for the annihilation of Amalek." He advanced two reasons for this. One was the need to ensure "racial purity." The other lay in "the antagonism between Israel and Amalek as an expression of the antagonism between light and darkness, the pure and the unclean."

For the Gush, there is a dimension to the settlements beyond the merely strategic—the defending of the state—or the territorial—the expansion of the "Land of Israel" till it reaches its full, biblically foretold borders. Settlements are the citadels of their messianic ideology, the nucleus and inspiration of their theocratic state-in-the-making, the power base from which to conduct an internal struggle that is inseparable from the external one—the intra-Jewish struggle against that other Israel, the secular-modernist one of original, mainstream Zionism, which stands in their path. The Gush must make good what Rabbi Kook taught: that the existing State of Israel carries within itself "the Kingdom of Israel, the Kingdom of Heaven on Earth; consequently, total Holiness embraces every Jewish person, every deed, every phenomenon, including Jewish secularism, which will be one day be swallowed by Holiness, by Redemption."

## Peace Is Not an Option

It goes without saying that the Gush consider any American-sponsored Arab-Israeli peaceful settlement to be a virtual impossibility; but furthermore, any attempt to achieve that impossibility should be actively sabotaged. For them, the Oslo Accords [promoting peace in the region], and the prospect of the "re-division" of the "Land of Israel," was a profound, existential shock. It was, said Rabbi Yair Dreyfus, an "apostasy" which, the day it came into effect, would mark "the end of the Jewish-Zionist era [from 1948 to 1993] in the sacred history of the Land of Israel." The Gush and their allies declared a "Jewish intifada" against it. The grisly climax came when, in the Ramadan of February 1994, a doctor, Baruch Goldstein, Israeli but Brooklyn-born-and-bred, machine-gunned Muslim worshippers in Hebron's Ibrahimi Mosque, killing 29 of them before he was killed himself. This was no mere isolated act of a madman. Goldstein was a follower of New York's Lubavitcher Rebbe. But what he did reflected and exemplified the whole milieu from which he sprang, the religious settlers, and the National Religious Party behind them. There was no more eloquent demonstration of that than the immediate, spontaneous responses to the mass murder; these yielded nothing, in breadth or intensity, to the Palestinians' responses to their fundamentalist suicide bombings, when these first got going in the wake of it. Many were the rabbis who praised this "act," "event" or "occurrence," as they delicately called it. Within two days the walls of Jerusalem's religious neighborhoods were covered with posters extolling Goldstein's virtues and lamenting that the toll of dead Palestinians had not been higher. In fact, the satisfaction extended well beyond the religious camp in general; polls said that 50 percent of the Israeli people, and especially the young, more or less approved of it.

The "Jewish intifada" also turned on other Jews. Yigal Amir, who assassinated Prime Minister Yitzhak Rabin in November 1995, was no less a product than Goldstein of the milieu from which the latter sprang. As in other religious traditions, the hatred Jewish fundamentalists nurtured for Jewish "traitors" and "apostates" was perhaps even greater than it was for non-Jews. Rabin, and the "left," were indeed traitors in their eyes; they were "worshippers of the Golden Calf of a delusory peace." And in a clear example of their deep emotional kinship with the fundamentalists, Sharon and several other Likud and far-right secular nationalist leaders joined the hue and cry against Rabin and his government of "criminals," "Nazis" and "Quislings." Declaring that "there are tyrants at the gate," Sharon likened Oslo to the collaboration between France's Marshal Pétain and Hitler and said that Rabin and his foreign minister, Shimon Peres, were both "crazed" in their indifference to the slaughter of Jews.

The struggle between the religious—in its fundamentalist form—and the secular, between ancient and modern, ethnocentric and universal, is a struggle for Israel's very soul. The Gush settlements are at the heart of it. The struggle is intensifying and is wholly unresolved. The fundamentalists can never win it; they are simply too backward and benighted for that. But, appeased, surreptitiously connived with, or un-ashamedly supported down the years by Labor as much as by Likud,[2] they have now acquired such an ascendancy over the whole political process, such a penetration of the apparatus of the state, military and administrative, executive and legislative branches, that no elected government can win it either. Meanwhile, they grow increasingly defiant, lawless and hysterical in pursuit of the millennium.

2. Labor and Likud are political parties in Israel

> "The legitimate demands of Israel can—
> and must—be reconciled with the
> human and political rights of
> Palestinian Arabs."

# Israeli Jews Work for Peace in the Middle East

## Liberal Judaism

*According to Liberal Judaism in the following viewpoint, Israeli Judaism is a force of good in the lives of the Jewish people, in the Middle East region, and for all humanity. The organization defends the state of Israel as a necessary haven for dispersed Jews. Liberal Judaism further contends that Israel can be secured from regional violence without sacrificing the rights of Palestinian Arabs. The organization concludes by affirming its commitment to the cessation of war, terrorism, and all forms of violence. Liberal Judaism is a Jewish organization working for social justice.*

As you read, consider the following questions:

1. Why is the reestablishment of a Jewish homeland a matter of urgent necessity, as defined by Liberal Judaism?

"Where We Stand, Zionism & Israel," www.liberaljudaism.org, 2005. Reproduced by permission.

2. According to the organization, what is Israel's greatest need?

3. What does maintaining a climate of opinion supportive of the quest for peace require of Jews, as stated by the authors?

We recognise the unique role which the Land of Israel has played in the history, prayers and hopes of our people through the ages. We also acknowledge that the discrimination and persecution, culminating in the Holocaust, which have so often been the lot of our people during the centuries of their dispersion, have made the re-establishment of an autonomous Jewish community in our ancient homeland a matter of urgent necessity. We therefore salute the Pioneers of Zionism [an international movement for the establishment of a Jewish state in Palestine] and the founders and defenders of the State of Israel whose vision and courage have turned that dream into reality. We reaffirm our love for the Land of Israel, our solidarity with our brothers and sisters who dwell within its borders, and our commitment to the State of Israel. We rejoice in its existence, delight in its achievements, care about its security, seek its welfare, believe in its future, and hope for the ever fuller realisation of the ideals set forth in its Proclamation of Independence, so that it may become more and more a force for good in the life of the Jewish people, of the Middle East region and of humanity.

We also reaffirm our faith in the Diaspora [the settling of scattered colonies of Jews outside Palestine]. In spite of the sufferings our people have experienced in dispersion, there have been nations which have welcomed Jews as citizens, and periods of Jewish religious and cultural creativity stimulated by close contact with other religions and cultures. Moreover, as a universal religion, Judaism is in principle at home anywhere on God's earth, and since it has a redemptive contribution to make to the life of humanity (to be 'a light to the nations'), it is positively desirable that there should be a Jewish presence in many lands. We therefore urge the importance of maintaining strong, confident and self-respecting Jewish communities in the Diaspora.

We endorse Rabbi Leo Baeck's perception of the Jewish people as an ellipse having two foci. Israel and the Diaspora have somewhat different roles to play, but they both exist for the same ultimate purpose, defined by Judaism, and should therefore be seen as equal partners in a common task. We desire to see a constructive relationship, of mutual respect, support and enrichment between Israel and the Diaspora. We believe that the Diaspora has the responsibility of sharing in the upbuilding of the State of Israel as a haven of refuge and a society where Jews can live in dignity and set an example to mankind:

We therefore urge our communities to continue and intensify all appropriate endeavours, including cultural activities, financial support for humanitarian purposes in Israel, and the encouragement of individual and group visits to Israel, towards that end. We believe that these endeavours should include the presentation of Aliyah [the immigration of Jews to Israel] as a noble option available to Diaspora Jews, and the encouragement of those who choose to seek their self-fulfilment, and to make their contribution to Jewish life, in that way.

However, we reaffirm our belief that full participation in Jewish life in the Diaspora, to ensure its continuation, is equally honourable. We demand full acceptance of the principle of religious pluralism, with all its implications, both in Israeli law and in the Zionist and communal organisations of the Diaspora. This requires that Progressive Judaism, as well as Conservative Judaism, be accorded recognition and respect, rights and opportunities, on terms of absolute equality with Orthodox Judaism. We regard this as a matter of justice, which is therefore independent of numerical considerations, and unnegotiable.

## Judaism Works for Freedom and Human Rights

If anyone doubts that religion can be a positive force for justice and peace, they need look no further than the work you [Religious Action Center for Reform Judaism] have done on religious freedom and other human rights, nuclear weapons, Third World debt and a host of other pressing issues. . . .

I thank God for the presence, in this national and international struggle for religious freedom and human rights, of the Religious Action Center of Reformed Judaism and of so many other faith-based Jewish organizations. Your role is essential and your accomplishments are legion.

*Theodore Edgar Cardinal McCarrick, "Address to the Religious Action Center for Reform Judaism," March 21, 2005. www.Cardinalrating.com.*

We believe that the Israel-Diaspora partnership requires mutual respect as well as open, candid and vigorous discussion of common concerns between the partners and within each. Such discussion should not exclude responsible criticism of particular governmental policies or other aspects of Israeli society, expressed with loving concern and due deliberation. For every possible reason, including its own long-term survival, Israel's greatest need is to 'seek peace and pursue it' (Psalm 34:15)

We recognise that there is room for a variety of views as to the best way of attaining that objective, but it seems to us self-evident that the whole ethos of Judaism in general, and of Liberal Judaism in particular, should incline us towards the view of those who would cede territory for lasting peace.

Reconciliation between Jews and Arabs is a goal towards which we strive. Concern for secure borders and political and military stability needs to be seen as compatible with justice for all. The legitimate security demands of Israel can—and must—be reconciled with the human and political rights of Palestinian Arabs. It is for all these reasons that we support the concept of territorial compromise. Our endorsement of these principles is in basic accord with a resolution adopted in 1984 by the Central Conference of American Rabbis (CCAR), the world's largest rabbinic assembly, with over 1200 members. We believe that we have a Jewish religious duty to foster, especially within Anglo-Jewry, a climate of opinion supportive of the quest for peace.

This requires us to keep ourselves well informed, to seek an objective understanding of the issues, and to exemplify and encourage the forces of moderation and reconciliation rather than those of strident partisanship. We applaud all sincere peace initiatives, and believe that such plans should always be sympathetically considered for their possible merits rather than rejected out of hand for their perceived inadequacies.

Likewise we welcome all contacts and conversations between the protagonists of the conflict in the Middle East and their respective supporters in Britain which may help to lessen tension, dispel ignorance, overcome mistrust, and build bridges of understanding. We call upon all States which have not already done so to recognise the State of Israel and establish normal relations with it. We ask all religious communities to try to understand the importance of the State of Israel for the Jewish people. We pledge ourselves to work together with all nations and religions for the achievement of peace in the Middle East, and for the cessation of war, terrorism and all forms of violence, the relief of suffering, and the establishment of justice, in all societies everywhere.

# Periodical Bibliography

The following articles have been selected to supplement the diverse views in this chapter:

Karen Armstrong, Susannah Heschel, Jim Wallis, and Feisal Abdul Rauf  — "Fundamentalism and the Modern World," *Sojourners*, March/April, 2002.

Shmuel Bar — "The Religious Sources of Islamic Terrorism," *Policy Review*, June 1, 2004.

Johann Hari — "Apocalypse Soon," *Independent on Sunday* (London), June 29, 2003.

Glen Hiemstra — "Future Peril: Will Religion Be the Death of Us?" *Futurist.com*, 2003. www.futurist.com.

Leela Jacinto — "Islam vs. Christianity in a Holy War?" *ABC News*, September 30, 2004. www.abcnews.go-.com.

Alex Perry and Nick Papadoupoulos — "India's Great Divide: Mounting Fury over Religious Discrimination by the Hindu Majority Is Triggering an Increasingly Violent Muslim Backlash," *Time International*, August 11, 2003.

Eric Schechter — "In the Name of the Koran," *Jerusalem Post*, September 12, 2003.

Christopher Shea — "Why Do Suicide Bombers Do It?" *Boston Globe*, July 3, 2005.

# For Further Discussion

## Chapter One

1.  Gregory S. Paul argues that religion is irrelevant in most modern societies, but Swami Swahananda argues that religion makes life meaningful in modern society. What do you think accounts for their differing points of view? Which view do you find more convincing, and why?

2.  Charlotte Watts and H.E. Javier Cardinal Lozano Barragan disagree about whether the Catholic Church is helping or undermining AIDs prevention efforts. Could both points of view be right? Why or why not?

3.  The Dalai Lama says that true religion promotes peace in the world, but Vanessa Baird argues that religion promotes violence. Do the authors have the same idea about what true religion is? Explain your answer. What aspect of religion does each author focus on in his or her arguments?

4.  George W. Bush and Amy Sullivan disagree about the success of faith-based initiatives. Which author do you believe presents the best evidence in support of his or her arguments, and why?

## Chapter Two

1.  John Esposito contends that Islam does not encourage aggressive wars; Daniel Pipes disagrees. Are their respective arguments based upon the Koran, history, or both? Which author do you think has the stronger argument? Explain.

2.  John Dear argues that Christ forbade war, but James Turner Johnson maintains that Christianity upholds just war. Which author relies more upon the New Testament?

Which author relies more upon other writings of church authorities? Can these conflicting points of view be reconciled? Explain.

3. Mahinda Deegalle argues that Buddhism forbids war. On the other hand, Tessa Bartholomeusz argues that defensive wars are permitted in Buddhism. With whom do you think the Buddha would have agreed, and why?

## Chapter Three

1. You have been presented with arguments pro and con regarding whether Intelligent Design is a scientific theory. What do you think are the key differences in the authors' opinions regarding what is necessary for a theory to be considered scientific?

2. Nancy Pelosi says that stem cell research is a gift from God while William Saunders says it violates God's laws. Which view do you find more convincing, and why?

3. Dean Hamer claims to have identified a genetic basis for spirituality, but Carl Zimmer says that the evidence for such a claim is weak. If Hamer's studies were replicated, would you be convinced that there is a genetic basis for spirituality? Why or why not?

## Chapter Four

1. Yousef al-Qaradhawi claims that the Koran permits martyrdom via suicide bombing, but Bernard Lewis says that it does not. Are there any circumstances under which you think suicide bombing could be justified for religious or political reasons? Explain.

2. Henry A. Giroux argues that Christian fundamentalism threatens democracy in the United States. However, Shmuley Boteach argues that Christian fundamentalism promotes moral government in the United States. Are democracy and moral government the same thing? Why or why not?

3. Amitabh Pal argues that Hindu fundamentalist violence threatens India, but Ashgar Ali Engineer argues that it is not a serious threat. Do the authors support their respective arguments with the same type of evidence? Which author has the more compelling argument? Explain.

# Organizations to Contact

**Acton Institute for the Study of Religion & Liberty**
161 Ottawa Ave. NW, Ste. 301, Grand Rapids, MI  49503
(616) 454-3080 • fax: (616) 454-9454
e-mail: info@acton.org
Web site: www.acton.org

The Acton Institute is named after the English historian, Lord John Acton (1834–1902), who is best known for his remark that "power tends to corrupt, and absolute power corrupts absolutely." The mission of the Acton Institute is to promote a free and virtuous society characterized by individual liberty and sustained by religious principles. To clarify the relationship between virtue and freedom, the institute conducts seminars and publishes books, monographs, periodicals, and articles, including ones pertaining to religion and government.

**American Association for the Advancement of Science**
1200 New York Ave. NW, Washington, DC  20005
(202) 326-6400
e-mail: webmaster@aaas.org
Web site: www.aaas.org

The American Association for the Advancement of Science is an international nonprofit organization dedicated to advancing science around the world. It opposes efforts to compromise or weaken the teaching of evolution. It has placed on its Web site resources concerning what it views as the scientific basis for evolution and the shortcomings of so-called intelligent design.

**Americans United for Separation of Church and State**
518 C St. NE, Washington, DC  20002
(202) 466-3234 • fax: (202) 466-2587
e-mail: americansunited@au.org
Web site: www.au.org

Americans United works to protect separation of church and state by working on a wide range of pressing political and social issues, including religion in the schools, religious symbols on public property, church electioneering, and religion in public life. Research and resource materials on these issues can be found on its Web site.

## Beliefnet

115 E. Twenty-third St., Ste. 400, New York, NY 10010
(212) 533-1400
Web site: www.beliefnet.com

Beliefnet is an independent multifaith e-community. Beliefnet's Web site provides information and news about a variety of religions and spiritual practices and the opportunity to participate in dialogue groups and prayer circles.

## Buddha Dharma Education Association

78 Bentley Rd., Tullera, via Lismore, NSW 2480
  Australia
e-mail: bdea@buddhanet.net
Web site: www.buddhanet.net

This nonsectarian Buddhist organization promotes the teachings of the Buddha. Its Web site has a search engine, an online magazine, information on various sects of Buddhism, and instructional materials for all age levels.

## Christianity Today International

465 Gundersen Dr., Carol Stream, IL 60188
(630) 260-6200 • fax: (630) 260-0114
Web site: www.christianitytoday.com

Christianity Today International believes that the Bible was inspired by God and is infallible. The organization publishes a number of well-respected Christian magazines, including *Christianity Today*. Its Web site also offers articles on topics such as war, evolution, and fundamentalism.

## Intelligent Design and Evolution Awareness Center (IDEA)
PO Box 17424, San Diego, CA   92177-7424
(858) 337-3529 • fax: (858) 569-8184
Web site: www.ideacenter.org

IDEA is dedicated to promoting awareness of scientific evidence that supports intelligent design theory. Its Web site has information concerning intelligent design and the debate between creation theory and evolution.

## The Organization of the Islamic Conference (OIC)
PO Box 178, Jeddah   21411
   Kingdom of Saudi Arabia
e-mail: info@oic-oci.org
Web site: www.oic-oci.org

The OIC is an intergovernmental organization of fifty-seven states that combine efforts and resources to safeguard the interests and advance the progress of their peoples and other Muslims in the world. Its Web site includes press releases and speeches on terrorism, conflicts affecting Muslim nations, and cooperation among Muslim nations.

## The Pew Forum on Religion & Public Life
1615 L St. NW, Ste. 700, Washington, DC   20036
(202) 419-4550 •  fax: (202) 419-4559
Web site: www.pewforum.org

The forum seeks to promote a deeper understanding of issues at the intersection of religion and public affairs. It provides information on this subject to national opinion leaders, including government officials and journalists. As a nonpartisan, nonadvocacy organization, the forum does not take positions on policy debates. Its Web site includes many articles on the relationship between religion and democracy, both in the United States and in Islamic countries.

## Vedanta Society of Southern California
1946 Vedanta Pl., Hollywood, CA   90068-3996

(323) 465-7114
e-mail: hollywood@vedanta.org
Web site: www.vedanta.org

The Vedanta Society is dedicated to Vedanta, the philosophical basis of Hinduism, but it also promotes the harmony of all religions. The organization's Web site provides a wealth of information and resources on Hinduism, Buddhism, meditation, religion, and spirituality worldwide.

**World Council of Churches, US Office**
475 Riverside Dr., Rm. 1371, New York, NY   10115
(212) 870 3260
Web site: www.wcc-coe.org

The World Council of Churches is an ecumenical organization that brings together more than 340 churches, denominations, and church fellowships in over one hundred countries and territories throughout the world, representing some 550 million Christians. The council's Web site includes articles about ecumenical and peace activities worldwide.

# Bibliography of Books

Richard Antoun          *Understanding Fundamentalism:*
                        *Christian, Islamic, and Jewish Move-*
                        *ments.* Walnut Creek, CA: AltaMira,
                        2001.

Karen Armstrong         *The Battle for God.* New York: Ballan-
                        tine, 2001.

John Bowker             *God: A Brief History.* New York: DK,
                        2002.

John Corrigan           *Religion in America.* Upper Saddle
and Winthrop S.         River, NJ: Pearson Education, 2004.
Hudson

Dalai Lama              *How to Expand Love: Widening the*
                        *Circle of Loving Relationships.* New
                        York: Atria, 2005.

Dalai Lama              *The Universe in a Single Atom: The*
                        *Convergence of Science and Spiritual-*
                        *ity.* New York: Morgan Road, 2005.

Noah Feldman            *After Jihad: America and the Struggle*
                        *for Islamic Democracy.* New York:
                        Farrar, Straus & Giroux, 2003.

Sam Harris              *The End of Faith: Religion, Terror,*
                        *and the Future of Reason.* New York:
                        Norton, 2004.

Bernard Lewis           *From Babel to Dragomans: Interpret-*
                        *ing the Middle East.* Oxford: Oxford
                        University Press, 2004.

Irshad Manji            *The Trouble with Islam.* New York: St.
                        Martin's, 2003.

Robert Pape             *Dying to Win: The Strategic Logic of*
                        *Suicide Terrorism.* New York: Random
                        House, 2005.

| | |
|---|---|
| Ted Peters and Gaymon Bennett, eds. | *Bridging Science and Religion*. Minneapolis: Fortress, 2003. |
| Michael Ruse | *The Evolution-Creation Struggle*. Cambridge, MA: Harvard University Press, 2005. |
| Huston Smith | *Why Religion Matters*. New York: HarperCollins, 2001. |
| Ray Takeyh and Nikolas K. Gvosdev | *The Receding Shadow of the Prophet*. Westport, CT: Praeger, 2004. |
| Jeffrey B. Webb | *The Complete Idiot's Guide to Exploring God*. New York: Penguin, 2005. |
| Linda Woodhead, Paul Fletcher, Hiroko Kawanami, and David Smith, eds. | *Religions in the Modern World*. London: Routledge, 2002. |

# Index

abortion, 135–36
abstinence, 36, 44
Access to Recovery, 50–51
Acton Institute for the Study of Religion & Liberty, 220
addiction, recovery from, 50–51
adultery, 204
adult stem cell research, 130, 135
affluence, 20, 21
Afghanistan, 71, 72, 187
Africa
    Christianity in, 25
    HIV/AIDS in, 41, 42, 45
    religious violence in, 157, 166
African Americans, rights of, 19
aggression, 88, 96
    wars of, 63–77
agnosticism, 23, 24
Ahmedabad (India), religious violence in, 199
AIDS. See HIV/AIDS
Algeria, religious violence in, 77
Aliyah, 213
Allah, 61
Amalek, annihilation of, 208
America. See United States
American Academy for the Advancement of Science, 122, 220
Americans United for Separation of Church and State, 220
anger, 29–30, 93, 99
anti-Semitism, 207
anxiety, recovery from, 15
al-Aqsa mosque, 205
Arabia, 73
Arab-Israeli conflict, 202, 208, 209, 215
Arabs, 169, 202, 207, 208, 211, 215
Arjuna (Hindu warrior), 61
armed force. See conflicts; war

Armed Islamic Group, 77
Asia, HIV/AIDS in, 41, 42
Assassins (extremist group), 76–77, 166, 167–68
atheism, 21, 23–24
at-one-ness, 144
    see also self-transcendence
Augustine, Saint, 85–89, 91
Australia, 24, 25
authoritarianism, 170, 171, 176
authority, 86–90

Babri mosque, demolition of, 191, 199–200
Bartholomeusz, Tessa, 101
behaviors
    genetic influences on, 151–52
    human, 146
    spiritual, 140
belief
    origins of, 139–53
    rates of, 21–27
    see also God, belief in
Beliefnet, 221
bellum, 87–88
    see also war
Benedict XVI (pope), 37, 38–39
Bhagavad Gita (Hindu scriptures), 61
Bharatiya Janata Party (BJP), 186–87, 191, 193, 194, 200
Bhivandi-Jalgaon (India), religious violence in, 199
Bible, 24, 61, 82, 221
Biden, Joseph, 192
bin Laden, Osama, 61, 64–65, 68, 72, 75, 77, 166, 178
biology, 115, 116–17, 119–20, 124, 140, 145
Blacks. See African Americans, rights of

blasphemy, 164, 169
Bombay (India), riots in, 200
books, holy. *See* scriptures
Boteach, Shmuley, 177
Botswana, HIV/AIDS in, 41
brain, mechanisms in, 145–46, 150
Brazil, HIV/AIDS in, 46
Buddha, Gautama, 31, 93, 95–99,
    103, 105, 106
Buddha Dharma Education As-
    sociation, 221
Buddhism, 14
    global problems addressed by,
        18
    God gene and, 143
    peace teachings in, 61–62
    war forbidden by, 93–100
        con, 101–108
Bush, George W., 74
    faith-based presidency of, 47–
        58, 173, 174–76, 178, 180–81
    policies of, 79, 82, 182–83
        in India, 186–87, 190, 192,
            194
    reelection of, 171–72, 177,
        178–80

California, embryonic stem cell
    research in, 131
Cambodia
    HIV/AIDS in, 42
    religious violence in, 94
Campaign to Stop Funding Hate,
    193
Canada, 25
caritas, 88
Catechism, Catholic, war teachings
    in, 89
Catholic Church, 23, 111
    embryonic stem cell research
        and, 134–38
    helps fight AIDS, 33–39
        con, 40–46
    war teachings of, 89, 91

cells (biological), 119–20, 136
Central Conference of American
    Rabbis (CCAR), 215
change, social, 19, 26
charity, 14, 97
chemistry, genetic, 145–47
children
    with AIDS, 34
    killing of, 74, 158, 160, 164,
        166
    of prisoners, 51–52
    rights of, 136–37
China
    HIV/AIDS in, 41
    traditional religions in, 14
Christianity/Christians, 15, 16, 75,
    138, 221, 223
    fundamentalists are threat to
        U.S., 170–76
        con, 177–84
    growth of, 14, 21, 22, 25
    Hindu conflicts with, 193
    Islamic conflicts with, 15, 157
    in Israel, 205
    in Japan, 24
    persecutions of, 157
    war forbidden by, 75, 78–83
        con, 61, 84–92
    *see also individual Christian
        denominations*
Christianity Today International,
    221
churches, 16, 223
    government grants to, 53, 58
    membership in, 22, 24
    mentoring programs in, 51–52
    war and, 82–83
    *see also* separation of church
        and state
civilians, killing of, 74, 77, 86, 162,
    164, 166
clergy, 24, 27
    Muslim, 160
    *see also* monks; rabbis

Clinton, Hilary, 50
communalism, 197–99, 201, 213
communication, 28, 31
communism, 20, 21, 23–24
compassion, 14, 29–32, 48–49, 79
  in Buddhism, 93, 99–100,
    103, 106
  in Christianity, 183–84
compassionate conservatism,
  54–55
competitive advantage, 146
  *see also* evolution
complex-specified information
  (CSI), 114, 115–17, 125
conception, human, 135–36
condoms, 36, 40–46
conflicts, 41, 63
  armed, 87
  religion as cause of, 15–16,
    30, 61–62
  resolution of, 98–99
  *see also* war
Congressional Caucus on India
  and Indian Americans, 192
Congress Party (India), 197, 198
conscience, formation of, 137–38
consciousness, 145–46, 152
conservatives, 56
  Christian, 22, 45, 170–72
  compassionate, 54–55
Constantine, 79
conversion, to Buddhism, 94–95,
  101, 104
Copernicus, Nicolaus, 111
covenant, Jewish, 206
creation, 26, 111–12, 135
creator, belief in, 24, 25–26
culture, 27
cupiditas, 88

Dalai Lama, The, 28
dar al-harb, 65, 160
dar al-Islam, 65

Darwin, Charles, 25, 116–20, 124,
  146, 156
  *see also* evolution
Day, Dorothy, 80, 83
Dear, John, 78
Deegalle, Mahinda, 93
defense, 90
  *see also* self-defense; war
democracy, 222
  Christian fundamentalism
    threatens, 170–76
    con, 177–84
  in India, 200–201
  secular developed, 20, 23–27,
    195
Democratic Party (U.S.), 54
depression, recovery from, 15
descent with modification, 123,
  124
  *see also* evolution
Dhammapada (Buddhist
  scriptures), 97, 98–99
Dharma, 101, 106–107
Diaspora, 212–14
diseases, recovery from, 15, 16
DNA, 150, 151
doctors, 112
Dome of the Rock (mosque), 205
dopamine, 146
drug abuse
  HIV/AIDS and, 41
  recovery from, 18, 54, 55
duellum, 88
  *see also* war
Dutugemunu (Buddhist king),
  104, 106–107

education, 20, 21, 38, 56
  Christian, 171–72
  in India, 197–99
  scientific, 122, 126, 127–28
Egypt, religious violence in, 77
Einstein, Albert, 111–12

embassies, U.S., bombing of, 166
embryonic stem cell research,
  saves lives, 129–33
    con, 134–38
emic, 94
End of Days, 205
Engineer, Ashgar Ali, 195
England, 197
enlightenment, 144
environment, 145
Episcopal Church, embryonic stem
  cell research and, 133
Esposito, John, 69
etic, 94
Europe, 25, 27, 169, 178, 181
  HIV/AIDS in, 41
  religious violence in, 16
evangelical Christians, 25, 170–84
evil
  punishment of, 89–91, 92,
    96–97, 100
  struggle against, 63, 69, 70–71,
    80
evolution, 24–26, 116–25, 128,
  139, 146, 156, 220, 221
extremism/extremists, 19
  Hindu, 200
  Muslim, 69, 72, 74–77, 157

faith, 14–15, 62, 201
  actions and, 18–19, 50
  origins of, 139–53
  science and, 111–13, 122, 126,
    131–32
faith-based initiatives, are better
  than secular programs, 47–52
    con, 53–58
faith-based presidency, 47–58, 173,
  174–76, 178, 180–81
family, 35, 38
fatwas, 77, 161
fertilization, human, 135
force. See conflicts; war

fossil record, 119, 123
Fox, Michael J., 137
France, 24
freedom, 137–38, 214, 220
fundamentalism, 156–215, 221
  Christian, 22, 170–84, 205
  Hindu, 21, 185–202
  Islamic, 165, 196
  Jewish, 202–15

Galilei, Galileo, 111
Gandhi, Mohandas K., 79, 80, 81,
  198
gender, inequality of, 41, 204
genetics, 123, 124, 135
  determines spirituality, 27,
    139–47
    con, 148–53
genocide, 94
Gentiles, 204, 206, 207
Germany, 23
Giroux, Henry A., 170
global problems, religious solutions to, 18–59
global warming, 18
God
  belief in, 14–16, 18–26, 112,
    133, 139–53
  as creator, 117, 118, 135–36
  laws of, 35, 136–38
  mercy of, 72
  of peace, 81
God gene, 139–53
Good Samaritan Foundation,
  37–38
Gospel (Bible), 82
government, 220, 222
  Christian fundamentalists in,
    170–84
  faith-based initiatives and,
    47–58
  HIV/AIDS and, 38
  war and, 85, 90

Western, 71
*see also* authority; democracy
Gujarat (India), violence in, 186–94, 200
Gulf War of 1991, 72
Gush Emunim (Israel), 205–10

hadith, 66
Halacha, 203–204
Hamas, 167
Hamer, Dean, 139, 148–53
Hanedim, 205
happiness, 29, 31, 98
hatred, 29, 75, 97, 98–100
health, 15, 36, 38, 48
health-care workers, 38
Hebrews, 61
*see also* Jews/Judaism
heritability, 123, 144–45, 151
higher power, belief in, 22, 23–24, 51
Hinduism, 14, 222–23
fundamentalism is threat to India, 16, 21, 185–94
con, 195–202
war teachings of, 61
Hindutva, 196, 199, 200
Hirst, David, 202
Hitler, Adolph, 19
HIV/AIDS, 33–46
Hizbullah (check on spelling), 167
holy books. *See* scriptures
holy wars, 19, 61, 170, 176
*see also* jihad; just war theories
homosexuality, 45, 151–52
Honduras, HIV/AIDS in, 42
honesty, 31
human beings
equality of, 14
nature of, 29, 30
origins of, 118, 134–37

spirituality of, 27
humanism, 25
human rights, 14, 94, 203, 208, 211, 214
Human Rights Watch, 46, 186, 188, 192
hunger, 18

illiteracy, 200, 201
income, 20, 21
India
Hindu fundamentalism is threat to, 16, 21, 185–94
con, 195–202
HIV/AIDS in, 41, 42
India Development and Relief Fund, 193, 194
Indonesia, HIV/AIDS in, 41
InnerChange, 55
innocents. *See* civilians, killing of
instincts, spiritual, 140
intellect, influence of, 27
intelligent design, 220, 222
is scientific theory, 114–21
con, 122–28
Intelligent Design and Evolution Awareness (IDEA) Center, 114, 222
International Islamic Front for the Jihad Against Jews and Crusaders, 65
International Religious Freedom Act of 1998, 190
intervention, military, 87–88
*see also* conflicts; Iraq War; war
intifada, Jewish, 209–210
intolerance, 15, 62, 75, 170, 171
in vitro fertilization, 130–31, 135, 136
Iran, 21, 68, 166
Iraq War, 15, 79, 81, 82–83, 176, 187
Ireland, 24

irreducibly complex structures, 114, 116–20
Islam, 15, 16, 222
  Christian conflicts with, 157
  defense of, 69, 70–71, 73–75
  fundamentalism in, 165, 196
  global problems addressed by, 18
  growth of, 14, 21
  laws of, 68, 76–77, 160, 164, 168–69
  war encouraged by, 63–68
   con, 69–77
  see also Koran; Muslims
Islamic Jihad, 65, 77
Islamists, 68
Israel, 159–60, 180–81, 183
  democracy in, 202, 203–205
  establishment of, 205–206, 208, 209, 211–15
  religious violence in, 157, 165, 167
Israel-Diaspora partnership, 214
Israeli-Palestinian conflict, 61, 157, 165, 208–209
Italy, 24

Jabalpur (India), riots in, 199
Jafri, Ahsan, 189, 192
Japan, 24, 25, 27
Jataka narratives, 96
Jesus Christ, 19, 31, 183
  divinity of, 22, 24
  peace teachings of, 61–62, 78, 79–80, 82
Jewish Kingdom, 203–205, 208
  see also Israel
Jews/Judaism, 157, 178, 183
  fundamentalism promotes violence, 202–210
   con, 211–15
  stem cell research and, 132
  war teachings in, 61, 75

jihad, 61, 63–77, 159–60
job-training programs, 57
John Paul II (pope), 37, 45, 81, 137
Johnson, James Turner, 84
John XXIII (pope), 136
justice, 14, 80, 214, 215
  wars to achieve, 84–85, 87, 88, 90
just war theories, 78, 82–92, 95, 101–103, 106–108

Kansas, science education in, 126, 128
Kenya, HIV/AIDS in, 42
Kerry, John, 174, 178, 181
Kharijites (extremist group), 76
Khmers, killing of, 94
kindness, 30, 31, 32, 95–97, 99
King, Martin Luther, Jr., 19, 79, 80, 83
Knesset, 204
Koran
  peace teachings in, 74, 76
  suicide bombing permitted by, 158–63
   con, 164–69
  war teachings in, 61, 69, 70, 72, 73, 76
Kurdish terrorists, 167

Labor Party (Israel), 210
laws, 36
  canon, 86, 89–90, 91
  of God, 35, 136–38
  international, 87, 89, 90–91
  Islamic, 68, 76–77, 160, 164, 168–69
  religious, 202, 203–205
  Roman, 85
Laxman Rekha, 201
Lebanon, suicide bombings in, 167

Lewis, Bernard, 164
Liberal Judaism, 211
Liberation Tigers of Tamil Eelam
  (LTTE), 102, 103
life, origins of, 114–21, 123–25,
  135–38, 156
Likud Party (Israel), 210
love, 28–32, 36, 48, 79–80, 88
loving-kindness, 95–97, 99
Lozano Barragan, H.E. Javier
  (cardinal), 33

*Mahavamsa*, 104–107
Mansoori, Mehboob, 189
marriage, 33, 35, 42, 45, 157
martyrdom, 158–63, 166
Massachusetts, social services in,
  58
materialism, 120–21, 183
measurement, scientific, 143
Mecca (Arabia), 73
media, 38, 77
meditation, 81
mentoring programs, 51–52
messiah, 183, 205–206, 208
Middle East, 16, 25, 202–215
millennium, 205, 210
miracles, 15, 48
molecular genetics, 123, 143
monks, 74, 101, 103–104
monoamines, 145, 146
Moore, Michael, 82
morality, 157
  absolute, 171–72
  degradation of, 18
  in Israel, 206–207
  laws of, 136–38
  political, 87, 92, 179–80
Moses, 31, 112
mosques, 51–52, 191, 199–200,
  205
Muhammad, 16, 31, 164, 167, 168
  war teachings of, 66, 70, 73

murder, 167
Muslim Brothers, 165
Muslims, 222
  Christian conflicts with, 15
  fundamentalist, 165, 196
  government grants to, 56
  Hindu conflicts with, 185–94,
    198–99
  Jewish conflicts with, 61, 204,
    209
  killing of, 158, 160, 166, 169
  numbers of, 14, 21
  war and, 61, 63–77
  *see also* Islam; Shias; Sunnis
mystical experiences, 146

National Human Rights Commission (India), 188
National Religious Party (Israel),
  205, 209
naturalism, 25, 120–21
natural selection, 115, 123, 146,
  152–53
nature, 25, 114, 115–17, 121, 141–
  42, 150
Nehru, Jawaharla, 197, 198, 199,
  200
neurobiology, 143
New Age beliefs, 24–25
New Testament (Bible), 61
Noah's ark, 112
nonbelievers, 22, 24, 25
  killing of, 67, 74–75
noncombatants. *See* civilians,
  killing of
nonviolence, 78–83
  Buddhist teachings on, 94–
    100, 103
nurture, 141–42

Old Testament (Bible), 61
ontogeny, 119
optimism, 139, 146–47, 152

order, wars to achieve, 84–85, 87, 90–91

Organization of the Islamic Conference, The (OIC), 222

Oslo Accords, 209, 210

pacifism, 79, 94, 98–99, 101, 103–104, 105

Pakistan, 157, 198–99

Pal, Amitabh, 185

Palestine
occupation of, 159–61, 165, 205–209
peace in, 211, 215
terrorists in, 167
see also Israeli-Palestinian conflict

Palestinian Islamic Jihad, 65

Pali Canon (Buddhist scriptures), 94, 95, 98, 99, 106

pan-Islamism, 165

patience, 30

Paul, (apostle), 86, 146

Paul, Gregory S., 20

peace, 28–31, 61–62
Buddhist teachings on, 99–100, 105
Christian teachings on, 80, 83, 223
Islamic teachings on, 69, 74
in Israel, 209–215
wars to achieve, 84–87, 90, 91–92

Pelosi, Nancy, 129

Pew Forum on Religion & Public Life, The, 222

pharmaceutical industries, 38

pharmacists, 176

Philippines, HIV/AIDS in, 43–44, 46

phylogenies, 119

Pioneers of Zionism, 212

Pipes, Daniel, 63

pluralism
in India, 195, 196, 201
in Israel, 213

Poland, 23, 25

politics, 24, 222
right-wing, 170–76
theories of, 85, 87, 92

Pol Pot, 94

Pontifical Council for Health Pastoral Care, 34, 37

poverty, 16, 18, 41, 200
elimination of, 56, 57, 201

practices, religious, 24, 28, 144

prayer, 15, 24, 81, 132, 144, 221

Presbyterian Church, 87–88

prisoners, counseling programs for, 51–52, 54, 55, 221

psychotherapy, Islamic-based, 15

public affairs, 221, 222–23

al-Qaeda, 72, 77, 192

al-Qaradhawi, Yousef, 158

Qur'an. See Koran

rabbis, 74, 204, 205

Rabin, Yitzhak, 209, 210

rationalism, 21, 25, 27

recidivism, 55, 56

reconciliation, 80

reductionism, 150, 171

Reeve, Christopher, 137

religion, 14–16, 220, 221, 222
decline of, 25–27
genetic role in, 139–53
global problems solved by, 18–59
is irrelevant, 20–27
con, 28–32
peace and, 28–32, 61–62
protection of, 197, 200
right-wing, 170–76, 186–87, 203

science and, 111–54
spirituality and, 143, 144
true, 32, 84
war and, 61–109
Religious Action Center of
Reformed Judaism, 214
religious correctness, 171–72
religious organizations, government grants to, 54–57
Republican Party (U.S.), 54, 174
respect, 14, 28, 31
retaliation, right of, 91
Revelation (Bible), 61
revelations, divine, 111
right-wing religion, 170–76, 186–
87, 203
Roman Catholicism. *See* Catholic
Church
Romans (Bible), 86, 90
Roundtable on Religion and
Social Welfare Policy, 56
Russia, 23
HIV/AIDS in, 42

Sabbath, observance of, 204
Sacred Island (Buddhist), 105–
106
   *see also* Sri Lanka, Buddhism
   in
Sadat, Anwar, assassination of, 68,
77
Sahib al-Bukhari, 66
Sangh Parivar, 200
Sanhedrin, 204
Saunders, William, 134
Scandinavia, 24
science, 22, 25, 26, 220
   religion and, 111–54
scientific method, 111, 124, 125,
143–45
scientists, 21, 38, 111–12, 124–26,
128, 133
scriptures, 61–62, 75, 111
   *see also specific holy books*

Secular Front (India), 198
secularism, 21, 23–27, 182, 195–
201
   in Israel, 208
selective advantage, 146–47
   *see also* evolution
self-defense
   in Koran, 63, 72, 73–74
   wars of, 88, 89–91
self-transcendence, 144, 145–46,
150–53
separation of church and state,
47, 49, 220–21
September 11, 2001, attacks, 19,
72, 157, 168–69
Sermon on the Mount, 82
serotonin, 146
settlements, Israeli, 205–10
sexual activity, 33, 35–36, 38, 42
sex workers, 41–45
Shah of Iran, overthrow of, 68
Shas party (Israel), 205
Shias (Muslim sect), 15
Sikhs, 199
sincerity, 31
Sinhala (ethnic group), 93, 99,
101, 103, 104–105
Sixth Commandment, 35
skepticism, 21, 22, 26
social services, 47–58
society, religious solutions for,
18–59, 97
souls, 136
South Africa, HIV/AIDS in, 41
Spain, 24
spirituality, is genetically
determined, 27, 139–47
   con, 148–53
Sri Lanka, Buddhism in, 93, 94,
101–108
stem cell research, 130, 133, 135
   *see also* embryonic stem cell
   research

Stem Cell Research Enhancement Act of 2005, 129

Sufis, 67

suicide
Islamic teachings on, 161–63, 164, 167, 168
prevention of, 15

suicide bombings, 158–69, 209

Sullivan, Amy, 53

Sunnis (Muslim sect), 15, 65, 77

supernaturalism, 21, 22

Swaziland, HIV/AIDS in, 41

Sweden, 24

Swift Boat Campaign, 174

sword verses (Koran), 74–76

synagogues, mentoring programs in, 51–52


Taliban, 72, 175

Tamil (ethnic group), 93, 103, 104–105

technology, 22, 25, 26

Teen Challenge, 55, 57

Temple, Jewish, reconstruction of, 205, 206

terrorism/terrorists, 18, 19, 61, 69, 72–77, 157, 222
suicide, 159, 166–68
see also bin Laden, Osama; war on terrorism

Texas, faith-based initiatives in, 54, 55, 57

Thailand, HIV/AIDS in, 43–44

theism, 26–27

theory, scientific, 124–25
see also scientific method

Theravada Buddhism, 94, 99, 106

Thomas Aquinas, Saint, 85–92

tolerance, 22, 30, 94, 95–96

trust, 28, 31

truth, 80, 97, 138

twins, studies of, 144–45

Uganda, HIV/AIDS in, 36

ulama, 75

umbilical cord research, 130, 135

unemployment, in India, 200, 201

Union of Orthodox Jewish Congregations of America, 132

United Nations, 178, 181

United Nations Programme on HIV/AIDS (UNAIDS), 33, 41, 45

United Presbyterian Church in the United States, 87–88

United Progressive Alliance (India), 198

United States, 222
Christian fundamentalism is threat to, 170–76
con, 177–84
Commission on International Religious Freedom, 189–90
Congress, 191
relations of, with India, 185, 186–87, 190–94
religion in, 20, 22, 24, 25–27, 47–52
religious violence in, 157
see also Bush, George W.; Iraq War

universe, origins of, 118, 125


Vanvasi Kalyan Parishad, 193–94

Vedanta Society of Southern California, 222–23

Vietnam, HIV/AIDS in, 41

violence, 72, 81–83
Buddhist teachings on, 93–107
in Islam, 75–77

Vishva Hindu Parishad (VHP), 200

VMAT2 (gene), 151, 152–53


war, 15–16, 18, 61–62, 87, 221
Buddhist teachings on, 93–108

Christian teachings on, 75, 78–92
Islamic teachings on, 63–77
necessities of, 158, 159–61
peace achieved by, 84–87, 90, 91–92
*see also* jihad; just war theories
war on terrorism, 88
Watts, Charlotte, 40
weapons, 86
women
 with HIV/AIDS, 41, 42
 killing of, 74

as suicide bombers, 167
World Council of Churches, US Office, 223

Yahweh, 61
youth, 24
 with AIDS, 34, 45
 in India, 201

zealots, 16, 171–72
Zimmer, Carl, 148
Zionism, 159–60, 205–208, 211, 213